BALLET PLOT INDEX

GARLAND REFERENCE LIBRARY
OF THE HUMANITIES
(Vol. 756)

BALLET PLOT INDEX
A Guide to Locating Plots
and Descriptions of Ballets
and Associated Material

William E. Studwell and
David A. Hamilton

GARLAND PUBLISHING, INC. • NEW YORK & LONDON
1987

Library of Congress Cataloging-in-Publication Data

Studwell, William E. (William Emmett), 1936-
  Ballet Plot Index.

  (Garland Reference Library of the Humanities; v. 756)
  Includes index.
  1. Ballet–Stories, plots, etc. I. Hamilton,
David A. (David Arnold), 1927- . II. Title.
III. Series: Garland Reference Library of the
Humanities; vol. 756.

GV1787.S75   1987   792.8′4   87-19758
ISBN 0-8240-8385-7

Printed on acid-free, 250-year-life paper
Manufactured in the United States of America

CONTENTS

PREFACE

Information about individual ballets is scattered throughout the extensive literature of ballet. This book is an effort to bring that scattered data together by comprehensively indexing plots and descriptions of individual ballets plus associated material such as illustrations, historical background, criticism and analysis, musical themes, and bibliographical references. Although formal plots and descriptions are the main focus of this publication, the wide spectrum of material covered makes the index to a considerable extent a general reference guide to individual ballets.

A variety of works wholly or partially of significant reference value, including sources for younger readers, were utilized. Excluded were dictionaries, encyclopedias, catalogs, and similar reference books on ballet and dance which typically have only a small amount of space, if any, dedicated to the stories and/or the action of the ballet. These reference books, however, are in some cases useful as a supplement to this volume. Altogether, 54 books in several languages (English, French, German, Danish, Russian and Polish, plus a translation from Italian) were indexed. Because of size and simplicity considerations, only one edition of each title was indexed, but the variations between editions were recognized.

The book is organized into five sections. First is a list of the sources indexed plus their codes as used in the main section, the ballet index. Second is a list of the codes for the associated material as used in the ballet index. Third is a detailed guide to the use of the ballet index. Fourth is the ballet index in which about sixteen hundred ballets, both directly composed and derived, from all western nations, of all periods, of all types, are listed along with the codes for the publications which have material on them. Entries for the ballets are made under the original title when known, except that titles in Russian, other non-Roman languages, or non-western languages are entered under their English or other western European language form when available. In case of doubt as to language, the English form is used. In case of multiple titles in the same language, the most common form is used. Cross references are made from other titles under which the ballet is known, including "or" variants. The composer(s) of the music is also given (unless authorship is unknown or too diverse, or there is no music), plus the earliest known date of the ballet's performance (unless the date is unknown). Normally, title was the criterion for distinguishing one ballet from another, but significant variations in plot and/or music also caused ballets to be regarded as separate entities. Fifth is the composer index in which all composers mentioned in the ballet index are listed, followed by the ballets with which they are associated.

DeKalb, Illinois
March 1987

SOURCES INDEXED AND THEIR CODES

ASC   Aschengreen, Erik. **Balletbogen.** Copenhagen: Glydendal, 1982.

BAI   Baignères, Claude. **Ballets d'hier et d'aujourd'hui.** Paris: Le bon plaisir, 1954.

BAL   Balanchine, George. **Balanchine's Complete Stories of the Great Ballets.** Edited by Francis Mason. Garden City, N.Y.: Doubleday, 1954.

BAM   Balanchine, George, and Francis Mason. **Balanchine's Complete Stories of the Great Ballets.** Rev. and enlarged ed. Garden City, N.Y.: Doubleday, 1977. (NOTE: Considered as a new title because of the addition of a second author.)

BAN   Balanchine, George. **Balanchine's New Complete Stories of the Great Ballets.** Edited by Francis Mason. Garden City, N.Y.: Doubleday, 1968.

BAO   Balanchine, George, and Francis Mason. **101 Stories of the Great Ballets.** Garden City, N.Y.: Dolphin Books, 1975.

BBP   Beaumont, Cyril W. **Ballets Past & Present : Being a Third Supplement to the complete book of Ballets.** London: Putnam, 1955.

BBT   Beaumont, Cyril W. **Ballets of Today : Being a Second Supplement to the Complete Book of Ballets.** London: Putnam, 1954.

BCB   Beaumont, Cyril W. **Complete Book of Ballets : A Guide to the Principal Ballets of the Nineteenth and Twentieth Centuries.** London: Putnam, 1937.

BCS   Beaumont, Cyril W. **Supplement to Complete Book of Ballets.** London: C.W. Beaumont, 1942.

BET   Bethléem, L. and others. **Les opéras, les opéras-comiques, et les opérettes.** Paris: Editions de la Revue des lectures, 1926.

BOL   **The Bolshoi Ballet : Ballet Company of the Bolshoi Theater of the USSR.** Moscow: Planeta Publishers, 1981.

BRI   Brinson, Peter, and Clement Crisp. **The International Book of Ballet.** New York: Stein and Day, 1971. (NOTE: Same as their **Ballet for All.**)

ix

BRU	Ballet russe de Monte Carlo. **Col. W. de Basil's Ballets russes (de Monte–Carlo).** London: Royal Opera House, 1936.]
CLA	Clarke, Mary, and Clement Crisp. **The Ballet Goer's Guide.** New York: Knopf, 1981.
CRB	Crosland, Margaret. **Ballet Carnival : A Companion to Ballet.** London: Arco, 1957.
CRT	Crowle, Pigeon. **Come to the Ballet.** London: Faber and Faber, 1957.
DAC	Davis, Jesse. **Classics of the Royal Ballet.** New York: Coward, McCann & Geoghegan, 1980.
DAS	Davidson, Gladys. **Stories of the Ballets.** London: W. Laurie, 1958.
DET	Detaille, Georges, and Gérard Mulys. **Les ballets de Monte–Carlo, 1911–1944.** Paris: Editions Arc–en ciel, 1954.
DOD	Dodd, Craig. **A Young Person's Guide to the Ballet.** London: Macdonald and Jane's, 1980. (NOTE: For younger readers)
DRE	Drew, David. **The Decca Book of Ballet.** London: F. Muller, 1958.
EWE	Ewen, David. **The Complete Book of Classical Music.** Englewood Cliffs, N.J.: Prentice–Hall, 1965.
FIS	Fiske, Roger. **Ballet Music.** London: G. Harrap, 1958.
GOO	Goode, Gerald. **The Book of Ballets, Classic and Modern.** New York: Crown, 1939.
GOU	Goulden, Shirley. **The Royal Book of Ballet.** Chicago: Follett, 1964. (NOTE: For younger readers)
GRU	Gruen, John. **The World's Great Ballets : La fille mal gardée to Davidsbündlertänze.** New York: Abrams, 1981.
HEA	Heath, Charles. **Beauties of the Opera and Ballet.** New York: DaCapo, 1977.
KER	Kerensky, Oleg. **The Guinness Guide to Ballet.** Enfield, Middlesex: Guinness Superlatives Ltd., 1981.
KOC	Kocho, Boris. **Diaghilev and the Ballets Russes.** New York: Harper & Row, 1970.
KRO	Krokover, Rosalyn. **The New Borzoi Book of Ballets.** New York: Knopf, 1956.
LAW	Lawrence, Robert. **The Victor Book of Ballets and Ballet Music.** New York: Simon and Schuster, 1950.
LAX	Lawson, Joan. **Ballet Stories.** New York: Mayflower Books, 1978. (NOTE: For younger readers)

MAY   Maynard, Olga. **The Ballet Companion.** Philadelphia: Macrae Smith, 1957.

MCD   McDonagh, Don. **The Complete Guide to Modern Dance.** Garden City, N.Y.: Doubleday, 1976.

PHA   **Phaidon Book of the Ballet.** Oxford: Phaidon, 1981. (NOTE: Has the same content as SIM but included because of different country of publication.)

REB   Rebling, Everhard. **Ballet von A bis Z.** Berlin: Henschel, 1966.

REG   Regner, Otto Friedrich. **Reclams Balletführer.** Stuttgart: Reclam, 1956.

REY   Reynolds, Nancy, and Susan Reimer-Torn. **In Performance : A Companion to the Classics of the Dance.** New York: Harmony Books, 1980.

REZ   Reynolds, Nancy. **Repertory in Review : 40 Years of the New York City Ballet.** New York: Dial Press, 1977.

ROB   Robert, Grace. **The Borzoi Book of Ballet.** New York: Knopf, 1946.

ROS   Roseveare, Ursula. **Selected Stories from the Ballet.** London: Pitman, 1954. (NOTE: For younger readers)

SEY   Seymour, Maurice. **Seymour on Ballet : 101 Photographs.** Chicago: Pellegrini and Cudahy, 1947.

SHE   Shelton, Suzanne. **Divine Dancer.** Garden City, N.Y.: Doubleday, 1981.

SIM   **The Simon and Schuster Book of the Ballet : A Complete Reference Guide, 1581 to the Present.** New York: Simon and Schuster, 1980. (NOTE: Has the same content as PHA but included because of the completely different title and the different country of publication.)

STO   **100 [Sto] Baletnykh libretto.** Moscow: Muzyka, 1966.

TER   Terry, Walter. **Ballet : A New Guide to the Liveliest Art.** New York: Dell, 1959.

TES   Terry, Walter. **Ballet Guide : Background, Listings, Credits and Descriptions of More than Five Hundred of the World's Major Ballets.** New York: Dodd, Mead, 1976.

TUR   Turska, Irena. **Przewodnik baletowy.** Kraków: Polskie Wydawn. Muzyczne, 1973.

UNT   Untermeyer, Louis. **Tales from the Ballet.** New York: Golden Press, 1968. (NOTE: For younger readers)

VER   Verwer, Hans. **Guide to the Ballet.** Translated from the Dutch by Henry Mins. New York: Barnes and Noble, 1963.

VIV   Viveash, Cherry. **Tales from the Ballet.** London: G.
          Ronald, 1958.
WIN   Winkler, H.J.   **Oper und Ballett.**   Munich: Südwest
          Verlag, 1964.

CODES FOR THE ASSOCIATED MATERIAL

(a) significant additional historical and/or analytic information

(b) one or more bibliographical citations

(i) significant illustration

(m) musical examples or themes

(x) no formal plot or description but of value because of illustration, analysis, historical information and/or other features

(!) especially important in this area

GUIDE TO THE USE OF THE BALLET INDEX

After each ballet title the following data is given in the order indicated:

1) the composer(s) of the music, plus the first known performance of the ballet, both in parentheses immediately following the ballet title;

2) variant forms of the title, including "or" variants, following asterisks (*). All name forms indicated are cross-referenced;

3) three letter mnemonic codes representing the sources in which material on the ballet is located, plus in many cases notation in parentheses indicating what kind of material, in addition to plots or descriptions, is included in the sources indexed. A list of the three letter codes and the sources they represent is given in the section "Sources Indexed and Their Codes," and a list of the notation in parentheses is given in the section "Codes for the Associated Material."

The two examples which follow are taken from the ballet index and cover all circumstances. Each element is diagrammed.

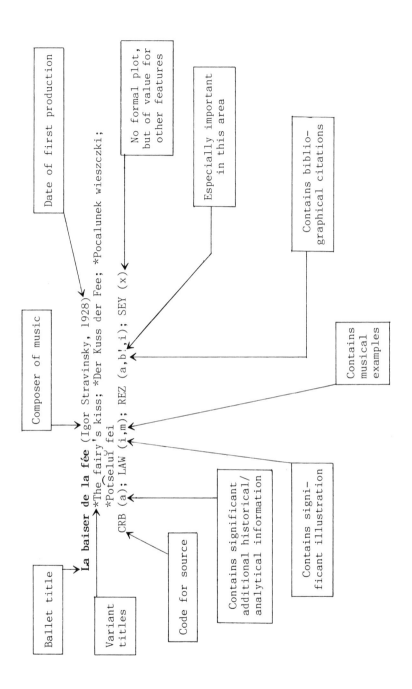

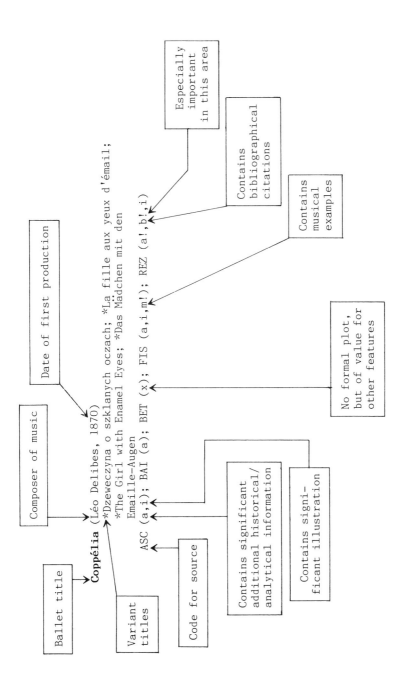

Ballet title

Composer of music

Date of first production

Especially important in this area

Contains bibliographical citations

Contains musical examples

Coppélia (Léo Delibes, 1870)
*Dzeweczyna o szklanych oczach; *La fille aux yeux d'émail;
*The Girl with Enamel Eyes; *Das Mädchen mit den
Emaille-Augen
ASC (a,i); BAI (a); BET (x); FIS (a,i,m!); REZ (a!,b!,i)

Variant titles

Code for source

Contains significant additional historical/ analytical information

Contains significant illustration

No formal plot, but of value for other features

BALLET INDEX

À la françaix (Jean Françaix, 1951)
    BAL (i); BAN (i); DRE; REZ (a,b,i); TER; TES

Åbenbaringer SEE Revelations

Abraxas (Werner Egk, 1948)
    BBT (a,i); REB (a!,i); REG (a,i); TRU (a); WIN

Abstraction SEE Somnambulism

Abyss (Marga Richter, 1965)
    BAM; BAN; TES

Acapulco (1963)
    MCD (a)

Accumulation, Primary Accumulation, Group Accumulation (1973)
    MCD (a,i)

Achille à Scyros (Luigi Cherubini, 1804)
        *Achilles at Scyros
    PHA; SIM

Achille in Sciro (Alessandro Rolla; Baigliù, 1806)
        *Achilles in Scyros
    PHA (a); SIM (a)

Achilles at Scyros SEE Achille à Scyros

Achilles in Scyros SEE Achille in Sciro

Acis and Galatea SEE Acis et Glathée

Acis et Galathée (Henri Durondeau; Luigi Gianella, 1805)
        *Acis and Galatea
    PHA (a); SIM (a)

Acrobats of God (Carlos Surinach, 1960)
    PHA (i); SIM (i)

Actus tragicus (Johann Sebastian Bach, 1969)
    TES

Ad Hominem (Zbigniew Wiszniewski, 1964)
    TUR (a,i)

Adagio Hammerklavier (Ludwig van Beethoven, 1973)
    BAM

Adam and Eve (Hilding Rosenberg) SEE Adam och Eve

Adam and Eve (Peter Sunthorpe) SEE In the Beginning

Adam och Eve (Hilding Rosenberg, 1961)
        *Adam and Eve; *Eden
    PHA (i); SIM (i); TES (i)

Adam Zero (Arthur Bliss, 1946)
    BBP (a,i); CRB; REG (a)

Adélaïde (Maurice Ravel, 1912)
        *Le langage des fleurs; *Valses nobles et senti-
        mentales
    BAN; DRE (a,i); LAW (m)

Aeon (John Cage, 1961)
    MCD (a)

After Corinth (David Gagne, 1975)
BAM

After Eden (Lee Hoiby, 1966)
BAM; BAO; PHA; SIM; TES

After "Suite" (1969)
MCD (a)

After the Time Before SEE The Time Before the Time After

Aftermath (Edgar Varèse, 1963)
MCD (a)

Afternoon of a Faun SEE L'après-midi d'un faune

Agamemnon's Return SEE Il ritorno di Agamennone

Age of Anxiety (Leonard Bernstein, 1950)
BAL (a); BAM (a); BAN; KRO (a); PHA (i); REZ (a,b!,i);
SIM (i); TER; TES

The Age of Gold SEE The Golden Age

The Age of Innocence SEE La prima età dell'innocenza

Aglaë (Johann Friedrich Keller, 1841)
*L'elève d'amour; *Love's pupil
BCB (a); PHA (a,i); SIM (a,i)

Agon (Igor Stravinsky, 1957)
ASC (a,i); BAM (a,i); BAN (a,i); BAO (a); BRI; CLA (a,i);
GRU (a,i); PHA (i); REB (a); REY (a,i); REZ (a!,b!,i);
SIM (i); TER; TES; TUR (a,i); VER (a,i)

L'ag'ya (Robert Sanders, 1944)
    CRB

L'aigrette (Georges Chavchavadzé, 1953)
        *The Egret
    DRE (a,i)

Aimez-vous Bach? (Johann Sebastian Bach, 1962)
    TES

Air and Variations (Johann Sebastian Bach, 1939)
    REZ (a,b,i)

Aistenok SEE The Little Stork

Alborada del gracioso (Maurice Ravel, 1944)
    BAM; REZ (b)

Aleko (Peter Il'ich Tchaikovsky, 1942)
    CRB; LAW (a,i,m); ROB (a,i); TER; TES

Alenka's Flower SEE The Blood-red Flower

Alen'kiǐ t͡svetochek SEE The Blood-red Flower

Alexander the Great (Phillippe Gaubert) SEE Alexandre le
        grande

Alexander the Great (Sergei Prokofiev, 1970)
    PHA (i); SIM (i)

Alexandre le grande (Phillippe Gaubert, 1937)
        *Alexander the Great
    BCB (i); PHA; SIM

Les algues (Guy Bernard, 1953)
    BBT (a,i); CRB

Alice in Wonderland (Joseph Horowitz, 1953)
    TER

Allegro brillante (Peter Il'ich Tchaikovsky, 1956)
    BAM; BAN; TER; TES

Alma (Giovanni Costa, 1842)
        *The Daughter of Fire; *La fille de feu
    BCB (a,i); PHA (a); SIM (a)

Alma Mater (Kay Swift, 1934)
    REZ (a,b,i)

Alye parusa SEE Crimson Sails

Les amants magnifiques (Jean-Baptiste Lully, 1670)
        *The Magnificent Lovers
    PHA (a,i); SIM (a,i)

Amor (Romualdo Marenco, 1886)
    BCB; PHA; SIM

El amor brujo (Manuel de Falla, 1915)
        *L'amour sorcier; *Czarodziejska miłość; *Der
        Liebeszauber; *Love, the Magician; *Love, the
        Sorcerer
    BAI; CRB; DET; DRE (a,i,m); LAW (i,m); PHA; REB (a);
    REG (a); SIM; STO

Amor di poeta (Robert Schumann; Rinaldi Rota, 1978)
        *Love and the Poet
    PHA; SIM

Amoras (Edward Elgar, 1940)
    DAS

L'amore delle tre melarance (Guilio Cesare Sonzogna, 1936)
    *The Love of the Three Oranges
    PHA; SIM

Amors og balletmesterens luner (Jens Lolle, 1786)
    *Les caprices du Cupidon et du maître de ballet;
    *The Whims of Cupid; *The Whims of Cupid and the
    Ballet Master
    ASC (a,i); BAM; BAN; BBP (a,i); BRI (i); PHA (a); SIM
    (a); TER (a); TES (a,i); VER (a)

Amour et Psyche (Vincenzo Manfredini, 1762)
    *Cupid and Psyche
    PHA (a); SIM (a)

L'Amour et son amour (César Franck, 1948)
    *Cupid and his Love
    BAL; BAM; BAN; DRE; TER; TES (a,i)

L'amour sorcier SEE El amor brujo

L'amour vainqueur SEE Les tentations de la bergère

Les amours d'Antoine et de Cléopâtre (Rodolphe Kreutzer,
    1808)
    BCB (a)

Les amours de Jupiter (Jacques Ibert, 1946)
    BBP (a)

An der schönen blauen Donau SEE Le beau Danube

Anaendrom (Jon H. Appleton, 1972)
    MCD

Anar (Vladimir Vlasov; Vladimir Fere, 1940)
    STO

L'anarchiste couronné SEE Héliogabale

Anastasia (Peter Il'ich Tchaikovsky; Bohuslav Martinů, 1971)
    BAM (a); BAO (a); CLA (a,i); PHA; SIM; TES

The Anatomy Lesson (Marcel Landowski, 1964)
    BRI

And Daddy Was a Fireman (Herbert Haufrecht, 1943)
    MCD (a)

The Angara (Andrei Eshpai, 1976)
    BOL (i!)

L'ange gris (Claude Debussy, 1953)
    BBP (i); DRE (i)

Angkor-Vat (Sol Cohen, 1930)
    SHE (a,i)

Les animaux modèles (Francis Poulenc, 1942)
    BAI (a)

Anna Karenina (Rodion K. Shchedrin, 1972)
    BOL (i!); PHA (i); SIM (i); TES

Annabel Lee (Byron Schiffman, 1951)
    BBP (i); CRB; TES

Anonymous (1959)
    MCD (a)

The Antagonists (Igor Stravinsky, 1955)
    MCD (a)

Antic Meet (John Cage, 1958)
    MCD

Antigone (Mikis Theodorakis, 1959)
    BRI

Antonia (Jean Sibelius, 1949)
    BBT (a,i); DRE

Apollo SEE Apollon musagète

Apollo, Herr der Musen SEE Apollon Musagète

Apollo i Dziewczyna (Ludomir Różycki, 1937)
    TUR (a)

Apollo i muzy SEE Apollon Musagète

Apollo, Leader of the Muses SEE Apollon musagète

Apollo placato (Louis de Ballou; Antonio Salieri, 1778)
        *Apollo Placated
    PHA (a); SIM (a)

Apollo Placated SEE Apollo placato

Apollo und Daphne (Leo Spies, 1936)
    REB (a)

Apollon musaget SEE Apollon musagète

Apollon musagète (Igor Stravinsky, 1928)
　　　　*Apollo; *Apollo, Herr der Musen; *Apollo i muzy;
　　　　*Apollo, Leader of the Muses; *Apollon musaget
　　　　ASC (a,i); BAI (a); BAL (a); BAM (a,i); BAN (a,i);
　　　　BAO (a); BRI; CLA (a,i); CRB; DET (i); DRE (a,i); GRU
　　　　(a,i); KOC (x); KRO (a,i); LAW (i,m); PHA (a); REB (a);
　　　　REG (a); REY (a,i); REZ (a, b!,i); ROB (a); SIM (a) STO;
　　　　TER; TES (i); TUR (a)

Appalachian Spring (Aaron Copland, 1944)
　　　　ASC (a); CRB; DRE (a); GRU (a,i); LAW (i,m); MCD; PHA;
　　　　REY (a,i); SIM

Apparitions (Franz Liszt, 1936)
　　　　BAL; BAM; BAN; BCB (i); CRB; CRT; DAS; DRE; PHA; SIM;
　　　　TER; TES

L'après—midi d'un faune (Claude Debussy, 1912)
　　　　*Afternoon of a Faun; *A Faun's Afternoon; *En
　　　　fauns eftermiddag; *Der Nachmittag eins Fauns;
　　　　*Popoludnie Fauna; *Prélude à l'après-midi d'un
　　　　faune
　　　　ASC (a,i); BAI (a); BAL (i); BAM (a,i); BAN (a,i); BCB
　　　　(a,i); BRI (a,i); CLA (i); CRB; DAS; DET (i); DOD (a,i);
　　　　DRE (a); GOO (a,i,m); GRU (a,i); KOC (x); LAW (i,m);
　　　　PHA; REB (a); REG (a); REY (a,i); REZ (a,b!,i); ROB
　　　　a,i); SEY (x); SIM; TER; TES; TUR (a,i); VER (i); WIN

Arcade (Igor Stravinsky, 1963)
　　　　REZ (a,b)

Arena (Morton Subotnick, 1969)
　　　　BAM

Armida's Pavilion SEE Le pavillon d'Armide

L'arrivée d'un nouveau seigneur SEE La somnambule (Louis
        Hérold)

As Time Goes By (Franz Joseph Haydn, 1973)
        BAM (a); BAO (a); CLA; TES

Aschenbrödel SEE Cinderella (Sergei Prokofiev)

Askepot SEE Cinderella (Sergei Prokofiev)

Assembly Ball (Georges Bizet, 1946)
        BAL; BAN; CRB; DRE; TER; TES

Astarte (Crome Syrcus Rock Band, 1967)
        BAM (a,i); BAO (a); BRI; GRU (a,i); TES (i)

L'astuce féminine (Domenico Cimarosa, 1920)
        *Le astuzie femminili
        DET (x); KOC (x)

Le astuzie femminili SEE L'astuce féminine

At Midnight (Gustav Mahler, 1967)
        BAM (a,i); BAO (a); CLA (i); TES

At the Cafe Fleurette (Victor Herbert, 1968)
        MCD (a)

Aubade (Francis Poulenc, 1929)
        DET (i)

Aureole (George Frederick Handel, 1962)
        ASC (a,i); BAM; MCD (a,i); REY (a,i); TES

Aurora's Wedding SEE Le mariage d'Aurore

Autumn Leaves (Frédéric Chopin, 1918)
    BCB (i); CRB; DAS; GOO (m); PHA; SIM

Et avisfrieri SEE Konservatoriet

The Baby Stork SEE The Little Stork

Babylon (Alexander Scriabin; Richard Wagner, 1937)
    SHE (a)

Bacchanale (Richard Wagner, 1939)
    BCS (a); CRB; GOO (i,m); LAW (i); ROB (a,i); SEY (x);
    TES

Les bacchantes (Alfred Bruneau, 1912)
    BET (a)

Bacchus and Ariadne SEE Bacchus et Ariane

Bacchus et Ariane (Albert Rousell, 1931)
        *Bacchus and Ariadne
    BAI (a); DRE (a,m)

Bach Sonata (Johann Sebastian Bach, 1970)
    BAM

Badinage (Johan Halvorsen, 1957)
        *Bergensiana
    TER; TES

Baïka SEE Le renard

Le baiser de la fée (Igor Stravinsky, 1928)
        *The Fairy's Kiss; *Der Kuss der Fee; *Pocalunek
    Wieszczki; *Potseluĭ fei
    BAL (a); BAM (a); BAN (a); CRB (a); DAS; DRE (a);

KRO (a); LAW (i,m); PHA (a); REB (a); REG (a); REZ
(a,b!,i); ROB (a); SEY (x); SIM (a); STO; TES; TUR (a);
WIN

Bajaderen SEE La bayadère

Bajaderka SEE La bayadère

Bajka (Ludomir Michal Rogowski, 1923)
    TUR (a)

Bakhchisaraĭskiĭ fontan SEE The Fountain of Bakhchisarai

Bakhtjisarajskij fontan SEE The Fountain of Bakhchisarai

Le bal (Vittorio Rieti, 1929)
        *The Ball
        BRU (i); DET (i!); GOO (a,i,m); KOC (x); PHA; SIM

Balance à trois (Jean-Michel Damase, 1955)
    PHA; SIM

Balerina (Georgiĭ Mushel', 1949)
    STO

The Ball SEE Le bal

Ballabile (Emmanuel Chabrier, 1950)
    BBT (a,i); DRE

Ballade (Claude Debussy, 1952)
    BAL; BAM; BAN; DRE; REZ (a,b,); TER; TES

La ballade de la géole de Reading (Jacques Ibert, 1947)
    BBP

Ballet comique de la Reine (Lambert de Beaulieu; Jacques
        Salmon, 1581)
        *Ballet comique de la Royne
    PHA (a,i); SIM (a,i)

Ballet comique de la Royne SEE Ballet comique de la Reine

Ballet de la délivrance de Renaud (Pierre Guédron; Gabriel
        Bataille; Antoine Boësset; Jacques Mauduit, 1617)
        *The Ballet of Renaud's Deliverance
    PHA (a,i); SIM (a,i)

La ballet de la nuit SEE Le ballet royal de la nuit

Ballet de la prospérité des armes de France (1641)
        *Ballet of the Prosperity of the Arms of France
    PHA (a); SIM (a)

La ballet des chevaliers français et béarnais SEE Le ballet
        des chevaliers françois et béarnois

Le ballet des chevaliers françois et béarnois (1592)
        *Le ballet des chevaliers français et béarnais;
        *Ballet of the Knights of France and Béarn
    PHA (a); SIM (a)

Ballet des échecs (1607)
        *The Ballet of Chess
    PHA (a); SIM (a)

Ballet des fées de la fôret de Saint-Germain (Antoine
        Boësset?, 1625)
        *Ballet of the Fairies of St. Germain Forest
    PHA (a,i); SIM (a,i)

Ballet des montagnards (Filippo d'Agliè, 1631)
*The Spirits of the Mountain
PHA (a); SIM (a)

Ballet du gris de lin SEE Il gridelino

Ballet Imperial (Peter Il'ich Tchaikovsky, 1941)
*Concerto No. 2; *Piano Concerto No. 2; *Second
Piano Concerto in G Major; *Tchaikovsky Concerto
No. 2; *Tschaikovsky Concerto No. 2
BAL; BAM (a); BAN; (BBT (a!,i); BRI; CLA (a,i); DRE (a);
KRO (a); LAW (i,m); PHA; REZ (a,b!,i); ROB (a); SEY (x);
SIM; TER; TES

Ballet mécanique SEE Iron Foundry

The Ballet of Chess SEE Ballet des échecs

The Ballet of Renaud's Deliverance SEE Ballet de la
déliverance de Renaud

The Ballet of the Disdainful Ladies SEE Il ballo delle ingrate

Ballet of the Fair Turks SEE Ballo di donne turche

Ballet of the Fairies of St. Germain Forest SEE Ballet des
fées de la fôret de Saint-Germain

Ballet of the Heiress of Bilbao SEE La douairière de
Billebahaut

Ballet of the Knights of France and Béarn SEE Le ballet des
chevaliers françois et béarnois

The Ballet of the Pope SEE Il Generale Colli in Roma

Ballet of the prosperity of the arms of France SEE Ballet de
        la prospérité des armes de France

Le ballet royal de la nuit (Jean de Cambefort; Jean Baptiste
        Boësset; Michel Lambert?, 1653)
        *Le ballet de la nuit
    BRI

Ballet School (Alexander Glazunov; Sergei Liapunov; Anatol
        Liadov; Dmitri Shostakovich, 1961)
        BAM; BAN; PHA; SIM; TES

Il ballo del Papa SEE Il Generale Colli in Roma

Ballo della Regina (Giuseppe Verdi, 1977)
        CLA (i)

Il ballo delle ingrate (Claudio Monteverdi, 1608)
        *The Ballet of the Disdainful Ladies
    PHA (a); SIM (a)

Ballo di donne turche (Marco da Gagliano, 1615)
        *Ballet of the Fair Turks
    PHA (a); SIM (a)

The Bandit's Daughter (Daniel Auber) SEE Marco Spada

The Bandit's Daughter (Cesare Pugni) SEE Catharina

Bar aux Folies-Bergère (Emmanuel Chabrier, 1934)
        *Bar of the Folies-Bergère
    BCB (a,i); CRB; DAS

Bar of the Folies-Bergère SEE Bar aux Folies-Bergère

Barabau (Vittorio Rieti, 1925)
     DET (i); KOC (x); PHA; SIM

Barbe-bleue SEE Bluebeard (Johann Schenck)

Barn Dance (David Guion; John Powell; Louis Moreau
     Gottschalk, 1937)
     BCS (i)

Une barque sur l'océan (Maurice Ravel, 1975)
     BAM; REZ (b)

Bartók Concerto (Béla Bartók, 1970)
     TES (i)

Bartók No. 3 (Béla Bartók, 1974)
     BAM; REZ (a,b,i); TES

Baryshniã i khuligan SEE The Young Lady and the Hooligan

Baryshniã-sluzhanka SEE Ruses d'amour (Alexander Glazunov)

Baśń krakowska (Michal Kondracki, 1937)
          *La légende de Cracojie
     TUR (a)

The Bat (Johann Strauss, 1936)
     REZ (a,b,i)

Eine Bauernlegende (Dieter Nowka, 1958)
          *Das Mädchen Hanka
     REB (a)

La bayadère (Léon Minkus, 1877)
          *Bajaderen; *Bajaderka; *Bayaderka; *The Dancing
     Girl; *The Kingdom of the Shades

ASC (a,i); BAM (a,i); BAN (i); BAO (a); BCB (a); BRI;
CLA (a,i); DAS; GRU (a,i); KER (a,i); PHA (a); REY (a,i);
SIM (a); STO (i); TES

Bayaderka SEE La bayadère

Bayou (Virgil Thomson, 1952)
DRE; REZ (a,b,)

Beach (Jean Françaix, 1933)
BRU (i); DET (i); GOO (i)

Beatrice di Gand (Adolphe Adam and others, 1845)
*Beatrice of Ghent; *A Dream; *Un Sogno
PHA (a); SIM (a)

Beatrice of Ghent SEE Beatrice di Gand

Le beau Danube (Johann Strauss, 1924)
*An der schönen blauen Donau; *Le beau Danube
bleu; *The Beautiful Danube; *Nad pieknym Dunajem
BAL; BAM; BAN; BCB (i); DAS; DRE (a); GOO (a,i,m);
LAW (i,m); REG (a); ROB (a); ROS (i); SEY (x); TES; TUR
(a); VER; WIN

Le beau Danube bleu SEE Le beau Danube

The Beautiful Danube SEE Le beau Danube

The Beautiful Pearl (Riccardo Drigo, 1896)
BBP (i)

The Beautiful Widow SEE Deuil en 24 heures

Beauty and the Beast (Thomas Hartmann) SEE The Blood-red
Flower

Beauty and the Beast (Thea Musgrave, 1969)
    BRI

Beauty and the Beast (Maurice Ravel, 1949)
    BAL; BAM; BAN; CRB (i); TES

The Beauty of Ghent SEE La jolie fille de Gand

The Bedbug (F. Otkazov; G. Firtich, 1962)
    *Klop
    STO (i); TES

Beggar's Dance (Johann Sebastian Bach, 1973)
    MCD (a)

Der bekehrte Spiesser (Dimitri Kabalevsky, 1953)
    REB (a)

La belle au bois dormant (Henri Dutilleux, 1953)
        *The Sleeping Beauty
    CRB (i)

La belle au bois dormant (Louis Hérold, 1829)
        *The Sleeping Beauty
    PHA (a); SIM (a)

La belle au bois dormant (Peter Il'ich Tchaikovsky) SEE The
        Sleeping Beauty (Peter Il'ich Tchaikovsky)

The Bells (Darius Milhaud, 1946)
    BBP (a,i); TER; TES

The Beloved (Judith Hamilton, 1943)
    MCD (a)

The Beloved One SEE La bien-aimée

Bereg nadezhdy SEE Coast of Hope

Bereg schast'i͡a SEE Coast of Happiness

Bergensiana SEE Badinage

Betty (Ambroise Thomas, 1846)
    BCB (a,i)

Bhakti (Ravi Shankar and others, 1968)
    BAM; BAO; PHA (i); SIM (i); TES; SIM

Les biches (Francis Poulenc, 1924)
        *The House Party; *Lanie
    BAI (a); BAL; BAM (a); BAN; BCB (a,i); BRI (i); CLA
    (a,i); CRB; DET (x); DRE (a,i); GOO (a,m); KOC (x); PHA;
    REG (a,i); REZ (b); SIM; TER; TES; TUR (a)

La bien-aimée (Franz Liszt; Franz Schubert, 1928)
        *La biene-aimée; *The Beloved One
    BCB; SEY (x)

La biene-aimée SEE La bien-aimée

The Big City SEE Grossstadt

Der Bilderraub SEE L'indifferent

Billy-dziecie SEE Billy the Kid

Billy Sunday (Remi Gassmann, 1946)
    TER; TES

Billy the Kid (Aaron Copland, 1938)
        *Billy-dziecie
        BAL; BAM (a,i); BAN; BAO (a); BCS (i); CLA (a,i); CRB;
        DRE; GOO (i,m); GRU (a,i); KRO (a,i); LAW (a!,i,m);
        REY (a,i); REZ (a,b!,i); ROB (a); TER; TES; TUR (a,i);
        UNT (i); VER

Biosfera (Marlos Nobre, 1971)
        BAM

The Birds (Ottorino Respighi; Constant Lambert, 1942)
        DAS

Birthday Offering (Alexander Glazunov, 1956)
        BAM; BAN; DRE; TER; TES

The Bitter Weird (Frederick Loewe; Trude Rittman, 1953)
        TES

The Bix Pieces (Bix Beiderbecke, 1971)
        MCD (a)

Black and White and Sparkle Plenty (Gabriel Fauré; Richard
        Strauss, 1966)
        MCD

Black Angel (George Crumb, 1973)
        *Black Angels
        PHA (a); SIM (a)

Black Angels SEE Black Angel

Black Swan (Peter Il'ich Tchaikovsky)
        SEY (x); TER; TES

Black Tights SEE Deuil en 24 heures

Blackface (Carter Harman, after Stephen Foster, 1947)
     REZ (a,b)

Blanche-neige (Maurice Yvain, 1951)
     BBP (i)

Blazen SEE The Buffoon

Bleecker to West 80th and Epilogue (Fernando; Syntonic
          Research, Inc, 1970)
     MCD (a)

Blind-sight (Bob Downes, 1969)
     BRI

Blomsterfesten i Genzano (Edvard Helsted; Holger Simon
          Paulli, 1858)
          *The Flower Festival at Genzano pas de deux; *Pas
          de deux af Blomsterfesten i Genzano
     ASC (a,i); CLA; GRU (a,i)

The Blood-red Flower (Thomas Hartmann, 1907)
          *Alenka's Flower; *Alen'kii tsvetochek; *Beauty
          and the Beast
     BCB; PHA; SIM

Blood Wedding (Denis ApIvor, 1953)
     CRB; DRE (m); TER; TES

Blood Wedding (Emilio de Diego) SEE Bodas de sangre

Blossoms SEE Duet for One Person
     MCD (a)

Blow-out (Wolfgang Amadeus Mozart; George Frederick Handel,
          1966)
     MCD (a)

Bludnyĭ syn SEE Le fils prodigue

The Blue God SEE Le dieu bleu

The Blue Train SEE Le train bleu

Bluebeard (Jacques Offenbach, 1941)
      BAL; BAM; BAN; BCS; CRB; DRE (a); KRO; LAW (a,i,m);
      PHA; ROB (a); SEY (x); SIM; STO; TER; TES

Bluebeard (Johann Schenck, 1896)
          *Barbe-bleu
      BCB; UNT (i)

Bluebird pas de deux SEE The Sleeping Beauty (Peter Il'ich
          Tchaikovsky)

Blues for the Jungle (Harry Belafonte; Oscar Brown, Jr.;
          Charles Mingus; Michael Olatunji, 1966)
      MCD (a)

Blues Suite (Pasquita Anderson; José Ricci, 1958)
      MCD (a)

Bodas de sangre (Emilio de Diego, 1974)
          *Blood Wedding
      PHA; SIM

Le boeuf sur le toit (Darius Milhaud, 1920)
          *The Ox on the Roof
      CRB

Bogatyri (Alexander Borodin, 1938)
          *Russian Heroes
      DET (i); DRE; GOO (a,i,m); LAW (a,i,m); TER; TES

The Boiled Egg SEE L'oeuf à la coque

La bôite à joujoux (Claude Debussy, 1919)
        *The Toybox
        DRE (a,m); PHA; SIM

Boléro (Maurice Ravel, 1928)
        ASC (a); BAI (a); CLA (i); DET (i); DRE (a); LAW (i,m);
        PHA; REB (a); REG (a,i); SIM; TER; TES; TUR (a); WIN

Bolt (Dmitri Shostakovich, 1931)
        TES

Bonne-Bouche (Arthur Oldham, 1952)
        BAL; BAN; BBT (a,i); CRB; DRE (a)

The Bores (Pierre Beauchamp) SEE Les fâcheux (Pierre
        Beauchamp)

The Bores (Georges Auric) SEE Les fâcheux (Georges Auric)

Boruta (Witold Maliszewski, 1930)
        TUR (a)

Les boucaniers SEE Jovita

Le bouffon SEE The Buffoon

Le bourgeois gentilhomme (Jean-Baptiste Lully, 1670)
        *The Would-be Gentleman
        PHA (a); SIM (a)

Le bourgeois gentilhomme (Richard Strauss, 1932)
        *The Would-be Gentleman
        DET (i!); DRE (i!); GOO (m); LAW (i,m); PHA; SIM; TER;
        TES

Bournonville divertissements (1977)
  BAM

Bourrée fantasque (Emmanuel Chabrier, 1949)
  BAL; BAM; BAN; BRI; DRE; KRO (a,i); REZ (a,b!,i); TER;
  TES (i)

La boutique fantasque (Gioacchino Rossini, 1919)
        *Czarodziejski sklepik; *The Fantastic Toyshop;
        *Im Zauberladen; *Der Zauberladen
  BAI (a); BAL; BAM; BAN; BCB (a!,i); BRI (i); BRU (i);
  CLA (i); CRB; CRT (a,i); DAS; DET (i!); DOD; DRE (a);
  EWE; GOO (a,i,m); KOC (x); LAW (i,m); PHA; REB (a); REG
  (a); ROB (a); ROS (i); SIM; TER; TES; TUR (a); VER;
  VIV (a,i)

Brahms Quintet (Johannes Brahms, 1969)
  BAM; BAO (a); TES

Brahms-Schoenberg Quartet (Johannes Brahms, 1966)
  BAM (i); BAN (i); REZ (a,b,i); TES

Brahms Waltzes, Opus 39 (Johannes Brahms, 1967)
        *Homage to Isadora
  BAM (a,b,i); MCD (a)

Brandenburg Nos. 2 and 4 (Johann Sebastian Bach, 1966)
  BAN (i); TES

Das Brauttüchlein (Jenö Kenessey, 1951)
  REB (a)

The Bright Stream (Dmitri Shostakovich, 1935)
        *The Clear Stream; *The Limpid Brook; *Svetlyĭ
        rucheĭ
  BCB; TES

The Broken Date SEE Le rendez-vous manque

The Bronze Horseman (Reinhold Glière, 1949)
        *Der eherne Reiter; *Mednyĭ vsadnik; *Miedziany
        jeździec
        BBP (a,i); PHA; REB (a); SIM; STO (i); TES; TUR (a)

Brouillards (Claude Debussy, 1970)
    BAM; TES

Bryllupet SEE Les noces

La buffonata (Wilhelm Killmayer, 1961)
    WIN

The Buffoon (Sergei Prokofiev, 1921)
        *Blazen; *Le bouffon; *Chout; *The Fool; *Der Narr;
        *Shut; *Skazka pro shuta
        DET (i); KOC (x); LAW (a,i,m); PHA; REB (a); REG (a,i);
        SIM; STO; TUR (a)

Bugaku (Toshiro Mayuzumi, 1963)
    BAM (a); BAN (i); REZ (a,b!,i); TER

Burlesque/Black & White (1967)
    MCD (a)

Bursztynowa Panna (Adam Świerzyński, 1961)
    TUR (a,i)

The Butterfly SEE Le papillon

Cadmus and Hermione SEE Cadmus et Hermione

Cadmus et Hermione (Jean-Baptiste Lully, 1673)
        *Cadmus and Hermione
        PHA (a); SIM (a)

Caesar in Egypt SEE Cesare in Egitto

Café des sports (Anthony Hopkins, 1954)
    CRB (i)

Café society (Ferde Grofe, 1938)
    BCS; GOO (m)

The Cage (Igor Stravinsky, 1951)
        *Klatka
    BAL (i); BAM (a); BAN (a); BAO; BBT (a,i); CLA (a); CRB;
    KRO (a); PHA; REY (a,i); REZ (a!,b!,i); SIM; TER; TES
    (a); TUR (a); VER

Cage of God (Alan Rawsthorne, 1967)
    BRI

Cagliostro w Warszawie (Jan Adam Maklakiewicz, 1947)
    TUR (a)

Cain and Abel (Richard Wagner, 1946)
    SEY (x)

Cakewalk (Louis Moreau Gottschalk, 1951)
    BAL; BAM; BAN; CLA (i); CRB; KRO (a); REY (a,i);
    REZ (a,b,i); TER; TES

Camargo (Léon Minkus, 1872)
    BCB; PHA; SIM

Camille (Franz Schubert, 1946)
    TER; TES

Cantata (Alberto Ginastera, 1974)
        *Cantata para América magica
    TES

Cantata para América magica SEE Cantata

Canto indio (Carlos Chavez, 1967)
    TES

Capital of the World (George Antheil, 1953)
    TER; TES

Capriccio brillante (Felix Mendelssohn, 1951)
    REZ (b)

Capriccio espagnol (Nikolai Rimsky-Korsakov, 1939)
        *Spanish Caprice
    BAL; BAM; BAN; BCS (i); DET (i); DRE; GOO (a,i,m); LAW
    (a,i,m); SEY (x); TER; TES (i)

Capriccioso (Domenico Cimarosa, 1940)
    TER; TES

Les caprices du Cupidon et du maître de ballet SEE Amors og
        balletmesterens luner

Caprichos (Béla Bartók, 1950)
    BAL; BAN; KRO (a); TER; TES

Capricorn Concerto (Samuel Barber, 1948)
    REZ (b); TER; TES

Capriol Suite (Peter Warlock, 1930)
    BAL; BAM (a); BAN; DRE; PHA; SIM; TER; TES

Caracole (Wolfgang Amadeus Mozart, 1952)
    BAL; BAN; DRE; REZ (a,b!,i)

The Card Game SEE The Card Party

The Card Party (Igor Stravinsky, 1937)
         *The Card Game; *Gra w karty; *Jeu de cartes;
         *Kartenspiel; *Kortspil; *Poker Game
    ASC (a,i); BAL (i); BAM (a); BAN (a); BBT (a,i); BRI;
    LAW (a,i,m); PHA; REB (a); REG (a); REZ (a,b,i); SIM;
    TER; TES (a); TUR (a); WIN

Carmen (Georges Bizet, 1949)
    ASC (a,i); BAL; BAM; BAN; BBT (a,i); BRI; CLA (a); CRB;
    DRE (i); PHA; REB (a,i); SIM; TER (i); TES (i); TUR (a);
    VER

Carmen suite (Georges Bizet, 1967)
    BAM; BOL (i!); PHA; SIM

Carmina Burana (Carl Orff, 1959)
    BAM (a); MCD (a); TES (i)

Carnation (1964)
    MCD (a,i)

Le carnaval (Robert Schumann, 1910)
         *Carnival; *Karnawal
    BAL; BAM; BAN; BCB (a,i); BRT; BRU (i); CRB; CRT (a,i);
    DAS; DET (i!); DRE; GOO (a,i,m); KOC (x); LAW (a,m);
    PHA; REB (a); REG (a); ROS (i); SIM (a,i); STO (i);
    TER; TES; TUR (a)

Carnival SEE Le carnaval

Carnival at Pest (Franz Liszt, 1930)
    BCB (i)

Carnival of Animals (Camille Saint-Saëns, 1943)
    DRE

Carrys (1969)
    MCD

Carte Blanche (John Addison, 1953)
    DRE

Casse-noisette SEE The Nutcracker

Castor and Pollux SEE Castor et Pollux

Castor et Pollux (Jean-Philippe Rameau, 1737)
        *Castor and Pollux
    EWE (a); PHA (a); SIM (a)

The Cat SEE La chatte

Catarina SEE Catharina

Catharina (Cesare Pugni, 1846)
        *The Bandit's Daughter; *Catarina
    BCB (a,i); PHA (a); SIM (a)

Catulli Carmina (Carl Orff, 1964)
    TES

Cavalry Halt (Johann Armsheimer, 1896)
        *Le halte de cavalerie; *Postój kawalerii; *Prival
        kavalerii
    BCB; PHA; SIM; TUR (a)

Cave of the Heart (Samuel Barber, 1946)
        *Medea; *Serpent Heart
    DRE (a)

Ce que l'amour me dit (Gustav Mahler, 1974)
        *What Love Tells Me
    PHA (i); SIM (i)

Celebration (1973)
    BAM (a); BAO (a)

Cellar (Wojciech Kilar, 1967)
    MCD (a)

Cello Concerto (Antonio Vivaldi, 1967)
    BAM

Cendrillon (Sergi Prokofiev) SEE Cinderella (Sergi Prokofiev)

Cendrillon (Fernando Sor) SEE Cinderella (Fernando Sor)

Les cent baisers (Frédéric d'Erlanger, 1935)
        *The Hundred Kisses; *The Princess and the
        Swineherd
    BRU (i); CRB; GOO (i,m); LAW; ROB (a); TER; TES

Ceremonials (Alberto Ginastera, 1972)
    TES

Ceremony (Krzysztof Penderecki, 1968)
    TES

Cesare in Egitto (1809)
        *Caesar in Egypt
    PHA (a); SIM (a)

Chabriesque (Emmanuel Chabrier, 1972)
    BAM; TES

Chaconne (Christoph Willibald von Gluck, 1976)
    BAM (a,i); CLA (i); REZ (a,b!,i)

Changeover (Mike Wodynski, 1973)
    MCD (a)

Changing Pattern Steady Pulse (Tim Ferchen, 1973)
MCD (a,i)

Changing Steps (Christian Wolff, 1973)
MCD (a)

Chansons madécasses (Maurice Ravel, 1975)
BAM; REZ (a,b!,i)

Chant du compagnon errant (Gustav Mahler, 1971)
*Song of a Wayfarer; *Song of the Wayfarer; *Songs
of a Wayfarer
BAM; PHA; SIM

Le chant du rossignol (Igor Stravinsky, 1920)
*The Chinese Nightingale; *The Nightingale; *Le
rossignol; *The Song of the Nightingale
BAL; BAM (a); BAN; DET (i); DRE (a); KOC (x);
LAW (a,m); PHA; REZ (a,b,i); SIM

Charade (Alwin Nikolais, 1966)
*Chimera
MCD

Charade (Trude Rittman, 1939)
*The Debutante
REZ (a,b,i); SEY (x)

The Chase (Wolfgang Amadeus Mozart, 1963)
*The Vixen's Choice
BAN; REZ (a,b,i)

La chatte (Henri Sauguet, 1927)
*The Cat
BCB (i); DET (i); GOO; KOC (x); PHA; SIM; TER; TES

La chaumière hongroise (Frédéric Marc Antoine Venua, 1813)
      *Les exiles célebrès; *The Hungarian Hut
   BCS

Checkmate (Arthur Bliss, 1937)
      *Schachmatt; *Szach-mat
   BAL; BAM; BAN; BRI; BSC (a,i); CLA (i); CRB; DAS; DRE;
   PHA; REG (a); TER; TES; TUR (a)

La chercheuse d'esprit (Charles Simon Favart, 1777)
      *The Spirit Seeker
   PHA (a); SIM (a)

Le chevalier errant (Jacques Ibert, 1950)
   BAI (a)

La chevalier et la damoiselle (Philippe Gaubert, 1941)
      *The Knight and the Lady
   BAI (a); BBP (a,i); CRB; PHA (i); SIM (i)

Chiarina (Boris Blacher, 1950)
   REG (a,i)

Children's Corner (Claude Debussy, 1948)
   DRE

Children's Games SEE Jeux d'enfants

Children's Tales SEE Les contes russes

Chimera SEE Charade (Alwin Nikolais)

Chinese Festival SEE Les fêtes chinoises

The Chinese Nightingale (Werner Egk) SEE Die chinesische
      Nachtigall

The Chinese Nightingale (Igor Stravinsky) SEE Le chant du
     rossignol

Die chinesische Nachtigall (Werner Egk, 1953)
     *The Chinese Nightingale
     REG (a,i)

Chopin Concerto SEE Classic Ballet

Chopiniana SEE Les sylphides

Choral Variations on Bach's "Vom Himmel hoch" (Igor
          Stravinsky, after Johann Sebastian Bach, 1972)
     BAM (a); REZ (a,b,i); TES

Choreartium (Johannes Brahms, 1933)
     BCB (i); BRU (i); DRE; GOO (i,m); LAW (i,m); ROB (a);
     SEY (x); TER; TES

Choreographic Miniatures (1959)
     TES

Choreographic Offering SEE Offrande choreographique

Choros (Vadico Gagliano, 1943)
     MCD (a)

Chota Roustaveli (Arthur Honegger; Nikolai Tcherepnin; Tibor
          Harsányi, 1946)
     BBP (a,i)

Chout SEE The Buffoon

Christmas Eve (Boris Asaf'ev, 1938)
          *Noch' pered rozhdestvom
     BCS

Chronica (Berthold Goldschmidt, 1939)
    BCS (a,i); DAS

Chung-Yang and the Mandarin SEE L'épreuve d'amour

Chung-Yang et le mandarin cupide SEE L'épreuve d'amour

Cimarosiana (Domenico Cimarosa, 1924)
    GOO (a,i,m); KOC (x); PHA; SIM

Cinderella (Frédéric d'Erlanger, 1938)
    GOO (m); ROB (a)

Cinderella (Sidney Jones, 1906)
    BCB (a)

Cinderella (Sergei Prokofiev, 1945)
    *Aschenbrödel; *Askepot; *Cendrillon; *Kopciuszek;
    *Solusjka; *Zolushka
    ASC (a); BAL (i); BAM (a); BAN (a,i); BAO (a); BBP
    (a,i); BBT (a!,i); CLA (a,i); CRB; CRC (a,i); DRE
    (a,i,m); GRU; KER (i); LAX (a,i); LAW (a,i); MAY (a!,i);
    PHA (i); REB (a); REG (a,i); REY (a,i); ROS (i); SIM
    (i); STO (i); TER; TES (i); TUR (a,i); VER; WIN

Cinderella (Boris Shel, 1893)
    *Solyushka
    BCB; PHA; SIM

Cinderella (Fernando Sor, 1822)
    *Cendrillon
    PHA; SIM

Ciné-bijou (Pierre Petit, 1953)
    TER

Circles (Luciana Berio, 1968)
    BAM; PHA; SIM

Circo de España (1951)
    TER

Circus Polka (Igor Stravinsky, 1942)
    BAM; DRE; REZ (b,i)

Cirque de deux (Charles Gounod, 1947)
    KRO (a); LAW (a,m); TER; TES

City Portrait (Henry Brant, 1939)
    REZ (a,b!)

Clarienade (Morton Gould, 1964)
    BAN; REZ (a,b); TES

Classic Ballet (Frédéric Chopin, 1937)
            *Chopin Concerto; *Concerto; *Concerto in E minor
    DRE; LAW (i,m); REZ (a,b,i); TER; TES

Classic Kite Tails (David Diamond, 1972)
    MCD (a)

The Clear Stream SEE The Bright Stream

Clearing (1967)
    MCD

Cleopatra (Anton Arensky) SEE Cléopâtre

Cleopatra (Paolo Giorza, 1858)
    PHA (a); SIM (a)

Cléopâtre (Anton Arensky with additions by Alexander
        Glazunov, Mikhail Glinka, Nikolai Rimsky-Korsakov,
        Sergei Taneyev, 1908)
        *Cleopatra; *Egipetskie nochi; *Une nuit d'Egypte
    BCB (a); CRB; DAS; DET (i); GOO (a,m); KOC (x); PHA;
    SIM; STO (i)

Cléopâtre, reine d' Egypte (Rodolphe Kreutzer and others,
        1825)
    BCB (a)

Clockwise (Jean Françaix, 1970)
        *L'horloge de Flore
    BAM; TES

The Closer She Gets...The Better She Looks (Herb Alpert,
        1968)
    MCD (a)

The Clowns (Hershey Kay, 1968)
    BAM; BAO; TES

Clytemnestra (Halim Ed-Dabh, 1958)
    MCD (a)

The Coach with the Six Insides (Teiji Ito, 1962)
    MCD (a)

Coast of Happiness (Antonio Spadavecchia, 1948)
        *Bereg Schast'ia; *The Happy Coast; *Shore of
        Happiness
    STO

Coast of Hope (Andrei Petrov, 1959)
        *Bereg nadezhdy; *The Shore of Hope
    STO (i); TES

Cobras (Léo Delibes, 1906)
MCD (a)

Collage III (Pierre Henry, 1958)
MCD (a)

Le combat (Raffaello de Banfield, 1949)
*The Duel
BAL; BAM; BAN; CRB; KRO (a); REZ (a,b!,i); TER; TES

Il combattimento di Tancredi e Clorinda (Claudio Monteverdi,
1624)
*The Fight between Tancredi and Clorinda
PHA (a); SIM (a)

Les comédiens jaloux (Alfredo Casella, after Domenico
Scarlatti)
DET

Commedia balletica (Igor Stravinsky, 1945)
*Musical Chairs
TER; TES

La commedia umana (Claude Arrieu, 1960)
*The Human Comedy
PHA; SIM

Common Ground (Michael Hobson, 1953)
CRB

Competition SEE La concurrence

Comus (Henry Purcell, 1942)
CRB (a)

Con amore (Gioacchino Rossini, 1953)
    BAL; BAM; BAN; CLA (i); CRB; DRE; KRO (a); REZ (a,b,i);
    TER; TES

The Concert (Frédéric Chopin, 1956)
        *The Perils of Everybody
    BAM (a); BAO (a); BRI; CLA (i); GRU (a,i); REZ (a,b!i);
    TER; TES

Concertino (Jean Françaix, 1950)
    REZ (b,i)

Concertino (Giovanni Pergolesi) SEE Concertino in A Major

Concertino in A Major (Giovanni Pergolesi, 1955)
        *Concertino
    REG (a)

Concerto (Frédérick Chopin) SEE Classic Ballet

Concerto (Edvard Grieg, 1953)
    DRE

Concerto (Francis Poulenc, 1969)
    TES

Concerto (Dmitri Shostakovich, 1966)
    BAM; BAN; BRI; CLA (i); TES

Concerto (Peter Il'ich Tchaikovsky, 1958)
        *Violin Concerto in D
    TER

Concerto barocco (Johann Sebastian Bach, 1941)
    ASC (a); BAL; BAM (a,i); BAN (a,i); BAO (a); CLA (i);
    DRE; KRO (a); LAW (m); PHA; REY (a,i); REZ (a,b!,i);
    SIM; TER; TES

Concerto for Flute and Harp SEE Mozart Concerto

Concerto for Jazz Band and Orchestra (Rolf Liebermann,
        1971)
    BAM (a); REZ (a,b,i)

Concerto for Piano and Winds (Igor Stravinsky, 1972)
    BAM; REZ (a,b)

Concerto for Two Solo Pianos (Igor Stravinsky, 1971)
    BAM

Concerto grosso (George Frederick Handel, 1971)
    BAM

Concerto grosso (Antonio Vivaldi, 1972)
    TES

Concerto in E Minor SEE Classic Ballet

Concerto in F Minor SEE Constantia

Concerto in G (Maurice Ravel, 1975)
        *Concerto in G Major
    BAM (a,i); REZ (a,b,i)

Concerto in G Major SEE Concerto in G

Concerto No. 2 SEE Ballet Imperial

Concierto de Aranjuez (Joaquín Rodrigo, 1952)
    DRE

La concurrence (Georges Auric, 1932)
        *Competition
        BRU (i); DET (i!); GOO (a,i); TER; TES

Confetti (Gioacchino Rossini, 1970)
        TES

Congo Tango Palace (Duke Ellington; Miles Davis; Gil Evans,
        1960)
        MCD (a)

The Conservatory SEE Konservatoriet

The Consort (John Dowland; Hans Neusiedler; Thomas Morley,
        1970)
        BAM (a); BAO (a); TES

Constantia (Frédéric Chopin, 1944)
        *Concerto in F Minor; *Konstancja
        BAL; BAN; DRE; ROB (x); TER; TUR

Les contes russes (Anatol Liadov, 1917)
        *Children's Tales
        BCB (a); BRU (i); DAS; DET (x); DRE; GOO (a,m);
        KOC (x); LAW

Contre (Luciana Berio, 1972)
        PHA; SIM

Contre-pointe (Marius Constant, 1958)
        TER

Les Contrebandiers SEE Stella

The Convalescent in Love SEE Il convalescente innamorato

Il convalescente innamorato (1784)
        *The Convalescent in Love
        PHA (a); SIM (a)

Coppélia (Léo Delibes, 1870)
        *Dziewczyna o szklanych oczach; *La fille aux yeux
        d'émail; *The Girl with Enamel Eyes; *Das Mädchen
        mit den Emaille-Augen
        ASC (a,i); BAI (a); BAL (a!,i); BAM (a!,i); BAN (i);
        BAO (a!); BCB (a,i); BET (x); BRI (a); CLA (a,i); CRB
        (i); CRT (a,i); DAS (a); DET (i!); DOD (a,i); DRE (m);
        EWE (a); FIS (a,i,m!); GOO (a,i,m); GOU (i!); GRU (a,i);
        KER; KRO (a,i); LAW (a,i,m!); LAX (a,i); PHA (a,i);
        REB (a); REG (a); REY (a,i); REZ (a!, b!,i); ROB (a!,i);
        ROS (i); SEY (x); SIM (a,i); STO; TER; TES; TUR (a,i);
        UNT (i); VER (a); VIV (a,i); WIN

Le coq d'or (Nikolai Rimsky-Korsakov, 1914)
        *The Golden Cockerel; *Zolotoĭ petushok
        BCB (i); CRB (i); DRE (a); GOO (a,i,m); KOC (x); LAW
        (i,m!); PHA; ROB (a); ROS (i); SEY (x); SIM; TER; TES;
        UNT (i)

Córka źle strzeżona SEE La fille mal gardée

The Corsair (1826) SEE Il corsaro

The Corsair (Adolphe Adam) SEE Le corsaire

Le corsaire (Adolphe Adam, 1856)
        *The Corsair; *Der Korsar
        BAM (a,i); BAN; BCB (a!,i); PHA (a,i); SIM (a,i); STO;
        TES (i)

Le corsaire pas de deux (Riccardo Drigo, after Adolphe
        Adam, 1899)
        *Korsaren; *Pas de deux af Korsaren
        ASC (a); CLA (i); GRU (a,i); REY (a,i)

Il corsaro (1826)
        *The Corsair
     PHA (a); SIM (a)

Cortège burlesque (Emmanuel Chabrier, 1969)
     BAM; TES

Cortège hongrois (Alexander Glazunov, 1973)
     BAM (a); REZ (a,b,i); TES

Cortège parisien (Emmanuel Chabrier, 1970)
     TES

A Costume Ball on Board Ship SEE Fjernt fra Danmark

Cotillon (Emmanuel Chabrier, 1932)
     BCB (a,i); BRU (i); DET (x); DRE; GOO (a,i,m); TER; TES

Could This be Death? SEE Serait-ce la mort?

Countdown (1966)
     MCD (a)

Country Houses (1963)
     MCD (a)

Couperin-suite SEE Verklungene Feste

Courante (Johann Sebastian Bach, 1973)
     TES

The Courtesan SEE Kurtisanen

The Courting at Burnt Ranch SEE Rodeo

Coverage (1970)
    MCD (a,i)

La création (1948)
    BBP (a,i)

La création du monde (Darius Milhaud, 1923)
            *The Creation of the World; *Die Erschaffung der
            Welt; *Die Schöpfung der Welt; *Stworzenie świata
    BCB (a,i); DRE (a); LAW; PHA (a); REB (a); REG (a);
    REZ (a,b,i); SIM (a); TUR (a); WIN

The Creation of the World (Darius Milhaud) SEE La création
        du monde

Creation of the World (Andrei Petrov, 1971)
    TES

The Creatures of Prometheus SEE Die Geschöpfe des Prometheus

Crimson Sails (Vladimir Yurovsky, 1942)
            *Alye parusa; *Red Sails
    BBP; STO (i)

Crises (Conlon Nancarrow, 1960)
    MCD (a)

La croqueuse de diamants (Jean-Michel Damase, 1950)
            *The Diamond Cruncher; *The Diamond Crusher; *The
            Diamond-muncher
    BAL; BAN; CRB; PHA; SIM; TER; TES

Crucifix SEE La damnée

Csizmás jankó SEE Little Johnny in Top-boots

A csodálatos mandarin SEE Der wunderbare Mandarin

Cuadro flamenco (1921)
     KOC (x)

Cudowny mandaryn SEE Der wunderbare Mandarin

Cupid and his love SEE L'amour et son amour

Cupid and Psyche (Lord Berners, 1939)
     DAS

Cupid and Psyche (Vincenzo Manfredini) SEE Amour et Psyche

Cupid Out of His Humor SEE Cupido

Cupido (Henry Purcell, 1956)
          *Cupid Out of His Humor
     TES

Cycle of Harmony SEE L'estro armonico

Cydalise and the Faun SEE Cydalise et le chèvre-pied

Cydalise et le chèvre-pied (Gabriel Pierné, 1923)
          *Cydalise and the faun
     BAI (a); BCB (a); LAW (m)

Le cygne SEE The Dying Swan

Cyrano de Bergerac (Marius Constant, 1959)
     TES

Czarodziejska miłość SEE El amor brujo

Czarodziejski sklepik SEE La boutique fantasque

Czerwony mak SEE The Red Poppy

Czerwony płaszcz SEE Il mantello rosso

Cztery eseje (Tadeusz Baird, 1961)
     TUR (a)

Czter temperamenty SEE The Four Temperaments

Dafnis i Chloe SEE Daphnis et Chloé

Daita (Georgiĭ Konius, 1896)
     BBP

Dalekaĩa planeta SEE A Distant Planet

La dame à la licorne SEE Die Dame und das Einhorn

La dame à la lune (Jean Françaix, 1958)
     TER

Die Dame und das Einhorn (Jacques Chailley, 1953)
          *La dame à la licorne; *The Lady and the Unicorn
     REG (a,i); TER

La damnée (Samuel Barber, 1951)
          *Crucifix
     CRB

Der Dämon (Paul Hindemith, 1924)
   WIN

Dance (1972)
   MCD (a)

The Dance Dream (Johannes Brahms; Alexander Glazunov; Peter
      Il'ich Tchaikovsky; Alexandre Luigini; Anton
      Rubenstein, 1911)
   BCB

Dance for Six, New Version (Antonio Vivaldi, 1969)
   MCD (a)

Dance in Two Rows, Version III (John Lennon; Paul McCartney,
      1970)
   MCD (a)

Dance Mania SEE Dansomanie

Dance of Steel SEE Pas d'acier

Dance of the Chosen SEE The Shakers

Dance Symphony (Ludwig van Beethoven, 1923)
         *The Magnificence of the Universe; *Tants simfoniĭa
   TES

Dances at a Gathering (Frédéric Chopin, 1969)
      ASC (a,i); BAM (a!,i); BAO (a!); BRI; CLA (i); GRU
      (a,i); PhA (i); REY (a,i); REZ (a!,b!,i); SIM; TES (a)

The Dancing-Girl SEE La bayadère

The Dancing School SEE Konservatoriet

Dancing with Maisie Paradocks (1974)
MCD (a,i);

Danse brillante (Mikhail Glinka, 1966)
TES

Danse concertantes (Igor Stravinsky, 1944)
BAL; BAM (a); BAN; BRI; DRE (a,m); LAW (m); PHA;
REZ (a,b!,i); ROB (a,i); SIM; TER (a); TES (a)

Danses polovtsiennes (Alexander Borodin, 1909)
*Polovetserdansene fra Fyrst Igor; *Polovtsian
Dances from 'Prince Igor': *Polowetzer Tänze;
*Prince Igor; *Tańce polowieckie
ASC (a); BAI (a); BAL; BAM; BAN; BCB; BRI; BRU (i);
CLA (i); CRB; DET (x); DRE; GOO (a,m); KOC (x); LAW
(a,m); REB (a); REG (a); ROB (a); TER; TES; TUR (a,i);
UNT (i); WIN

Danses slaves et tziganes (Alexander Dargomizhsky, 1936)
*Gypsy Dances
BRU (i); GOO (m)

Dansomanie (Etienne Nicholas Méhul, 1800)
*Dance Mania
PHA (a); SIM (a)

Dante sonata (Franz Liszt, 1940)
BAL; BAM; BAN; BCS (i); DRE (a,i); TER; TES; TUR (a)

Danza a quattro (Gaetano Donizetti, 1973)
TES

Daphnis and Chloe SEE Daphnis et Chloé

Daphnis et Chloé (Maurice Ravel, 1912)
*Dafnis i Chloe; *Daphnis and Chloe; *Daphnis og
Chloé; *Daphnis und Chloë
ASC (a); BAI (a); BAL; BAM (a,i); BAN (a); BCB; BRI;
CRB; DAS; DET (i); DRE (a,i,m); FIS (a,i,m!); GOO (m);

KOC (x); KRO (a,i); LAW (a,i,m!); PHA; REB (a); REG
(a); REZ (a,b); SIM; STO; TER; TES (i); TUR (a,i); VIV
(a,i); WIN

Daphnis og Chloé SEE Daphnis et Chloé

Daphnis und Chlöe SEE Daphnis et Chloé

Dark Elegies (Gustav Mahler, 1937)
    BAM (a); BAO (a); BAN; BRI; CLA (i); DRE (i); LAW
    (a,i,m); PHA; ROB (a,i); SIM; TER; TES

Dark Meadow (Carlos Cháves, 1946)
    MCD (a)

Daughter of Castille (Reinhold Glière, 1955)
    *Doch' kastiliĭ; *Eine Tochter Kastiliens
    REB (a)

The Daughter of Fire SEE Alma

The Daughter of Pharaoh (Cesare Pugni, 1862)
    *Doch' Faraona; *Dotch Faraona; *La fille du
    Pharaon; *Pharoah's Daughter
    BCB (a); PHA; SIM

The Daughter of the Danube SEE La fille du Danube

David (Maurice Jacobson, 1935)
    BCB (a);

David triomphant (Claude Debussy; Modeste Moussorgsky; Serge
        Lifar; Vittorio Rieti, 1936)
    BCB (i)

Davidsbündlertänze (Robert Schumann, 1980)
        *Robert Schumann's Davidsbündlertänze
    CLA (a,i); GRU (a,i)

Davo u selu (Fran Lhotka, 1935)
        *The Devil in the Village; *Der Teufel im Dorf
    BBP; DRE (a); REB (a); REG (a,i); WIN

Day on earth (Aaron Copland, 1947)
    MCD (a); TES

Death and the Maiden (Franz Schubert, 1937)
    DRE (a,i); TER; TES

Death of Adonis (Benjamin Godard, 1923)
    MCD (a)

The Death of Cleopatra SEE La morte di Cleopatra

Deaths and Entrances (Hunter Johnson, 1943)
    MCD (a,i)

The Débutante (Cuthbert Clarke; G.J.M. Glaser, 1906)
    BCB

The Debutante (Trude Rittman) SEE Charade (Trude Rittman)

Le déjeuner sur l'herbe (Joseph Lanner, 1945)
        *Picnic
    CRB

Del amor y de muerte (Enrique Granados, 1949)
        *Of Love and Death
    BAL; BAN; BBT (a,i); CRB; TER

Les demoiselles de la nuit (Jean Françaix, 1948)
        *Die jungen Damen der Nacht; *Ein Katzen-Ballet;
        *The Ladies of Midnight; *Ladies of the Night
    BAL; BAM (a); BAN; BBT (a,i); CRB; REB (a); TER; TES;
    WIN

Le départ d'Enée (Gasparo Angiolini, 1766)
        *The Departure of Aneas; *Dido Abandoned; *La
        Didon abondonée
    PHA (a); SIM (a)

The Departure of Aneas SEE Le départ d'Enée

The Descent of Hebe (Ernest Bloch, 1935)
    BCB (i); DAS

Designs with Strings (Peter Il'ich Tchaikovsky, 1948)
    BAM; BAN; BRI; KRO (a); TER; TES

The Desperate Heart (Bernardo Segall, 1943)
    MCD (a)

Despertar (Carlos Fariñas, 1954)
        *Erwachen
    REB (a)

Destiny SEE Les prèsages

Deuce coupe (The Beach Boys, 1973)
    BAM (a); BAO (a); GRU (a,i); MCD (a)

Deuil en 24 heures (Maurice Thiriet, 1953)
        *The Beautiful Widow; *Black tights; *Mourning
        Orders in 24 Hours
    BBT (a,i); CRB; PHA; SIM: TER

Les deux créoles (Jean Durondeau, 1806)
　　　*The Two Creoles
　　BCB (a); PHA (a); SIM (a)

Les deux pigeons (André Messager, 1886)
　　　*The Two Pigeons
　　BAI (a); BAM; BAN; BCB (a); BET; BRI; CLA (i); KER (i);
　　TES

Devich'iã bashniã SEE The Maiden's Tower

The Devil in Love SEE Le diable amoureaux

The Devil in the Village SEE Davo u selu

The Devil on Two Sticks SEE Le diable boiteux

The Devil to Pay SEE Le diable à quatre

The Devil's Bride SEE La fiancée du diable

The Devil's Fiancée SEE La fiancée du diable

Devil's Holiday (Vincenzo Tomassini, 1939)
　　GOO (i); ROB (a,i); SEY (x); TER; TES

The Devil's Violin SEE Le violon du diable

Le diable à quatre (Adolphe Adam, 1845)
　　　*The Devil to Pay
　　BCB (i); PHA (a); SIM (a); TES (i)

Le diable amoureaux (François Benoist; Napoléon-Henri Réber, 1840)
  *The Devil in Love
    BCB (a,i)

Le diable boiteux (Casimir Gide, 1836)
      *The Devil on Two Sticks
    BCB (a); HEA (a,i!); PHA (a); SIM (a)

Dialog (Michael Czajkowski, 1967)
    MCD (a)

The Diamond Cruncher SEE La croqueuse de diamants

The Diamond Crusher SEE La croqueuse des diamants

The Diamond-muncher SEE La croqueuse de diamants

Diana's Nymph SEE Sylvia

Diavolina (Cesare Pugni, 1863)
    BCB (a)

Dichterliebe (Robert Schumann, 1972)
    TES

Dido Abandoned SEE Le départ d'Enée

La Didon abandonée SEE Le départ d'Enée

Diener zweier Herren (Jarmil Burghauser, 1958)
    REB (a)

Le dieu bleu (Reynaldo Hahn, 1912)
   *The Blue God
   DET (i); KOC (x); PHA; SIM

Le dieu et la bayadère (Daniel Auber, 1830)
      *The God and the Bayadere; *The Maid of Cashmere
   BCB (a,i); PHA (a,i); SIM (a,i)

Les dieux mendiants SEE The Gods Go A-begging

Dim Lustre (Richard Strauss, 1943)
   BAM; BAN; CRB; DRE; KRO (a,i); LAW (i); REZ (a,b,i);
   ROB (a); TER; TES

A Distant Planet (Boris Maĭzel', 1963)
   *Dalekaĭa planeta
   STO (i); TES

District Storyville (Dorothea Freitag; Sidney Bechet; Duke
      Ellington; Jelly Roll Morton, 1962)
   MCD (a)

Diversion of Angels (Norman Dello Joio, 1948)
   MCD (a)

Divertimento (Alexei Haieff, 1947)
   BAL (i); BAN; REZ (a,b!,i); TER; TES

Divertimento (Gioacchino Rossini, 1941)
   REZ (a,b,i)

Divertimento from "Le baiser de la fée" (Igor Stravinsky,
      1972)
   REZ (a,b!,i)

Divertimento No. 15 (Wolfgang Amadeus Mozart, 1956)
   BAM (a); BAN; REZ (a,b,i); TER; TES

Doch' Faraona SEE The Daughter of Pharaoh

Doch kastiliĭ SEE Daughter of Castille

Doctor Aibolit (Igor Morozov, 1947)
        *Doktor Aĭbolit; *Doktor Au-Weh-Weh
    REB (a); STO

Dǿdens triumf (Thomas Koppel, 1971)
        *The Triumph of Death
    ASC (a,i); BAM; PHA; SIM; TES (a,i)

Den dǿende svane SEE The Dying Swan

Doktor Aĭbolit SEE Doctor Aibolit

Doktor Au-Weh-Weh SEE Doctor Aibolit

Don Domingo (Silvestre Revueltas, 1942)
    TER

Don Juan (Christoph Willibald von Gluck, 1761)
        *Le festin de Pierre; *Kamienny gość; *Der
        steinerne Gast
    BCB (a,i); DET (i); GOO (a,i,m); LAW (a,i,m); PHA
    (a!,i); REB (a); REG (a,i); ROB (a); SIM (a!, i); TER;
    TES; TUR (a)

Don Juan (Christoph Willibald von Gluck; Tomás Luis de
        Victoria, 1972)
    BAM (a); PHA; SIM

Don Juan (Richard Strauss, 1938)
    CRB

Don Kichot SEE Don Quixote (Léon Minkus)

Don Kikhot SEE Don Quixote (Léon Minkus)

Don Quichotte SEE Don Quixote (Léon Minkus)

Don Quixote (Roberto Gerhard, 1950)
    BBT (a,i); CRB; DRE (a,m)

Don Quixote (Léon Minkus, 1869)
        *Don Kichot; *Don Kikhot; *Don Quichotte
    ASC (a,i); BAM (a,i); BAN (i); BAO (a); BCB (a); BOL
    (a,i!); CLA (i); DRE; GRU (a,i); KER (a); PHA; REY
    (a,i); SEY (x); SIM (a,i) STO; TER; TES (a,i); TUR
    (a,i); VER (a)

Don Quixote (Nicolas Nabokov, 1965)
    BAN (a); BRI; REZ (a!,b!,i)

Don Quixote (Leo Spies, 1949)
    REB (a); REG (a)

Don-Zhuan (Leonid Feĭgin, 1964)
    STO

Doña Ines de Castro (Antonio Cortesi and others, 1827)
        *Ines di Castro
    PHA (a); SIM (a)

Doña Ines de Castro (Joaquin Serra, 1952)
    BBT (a,i); DRE (i)

Donald of the Burthens (Ian Whyte, 1951)
    BAL; BAN; BBP (a,i); CRB; TER; TES

Donizetti Variations SEE Variations from "Don Sebastian"

Le donne di buon umore SEE Les femmes de bonne humeur

Dornröschen SEE The Sleeping Beauty (Peter Il'ich
    Tchaikovsky)

Dotch Faraona SEE The Daughter of Pharaoh

La douairière de Billebahaut (Antoine Boësset; François
    Richard; Paul Auger, 1626)
    *Ballet of the Heiress of Bilbao
    SIM (a,i); PHA (a,i)

Double Concerto (Johann Sebastian Bach, 1964)
    MCD

Double Exposure (Alexander Scriabin, 1972
    TES

Dougla (Geoffrey Holder, 1974)
    BAM

A Dream SEE Beatrice di Gand

The Dream (Felix Mendelssohn, 1964)
    *Sen
    BAM (a); BAN; BAO (a); BRI; CLA; GRU (a,i); TES (i);
    TUR (a)

Dream Pictures SEE Drømmebilleder

A Dream Under a Black Hat (1971)
    MCD (a)

Dreams (George Antheil) SEE Songes

Dreams (Ralph Gilbert, 1946)
    MCD (a)

Der Dreispitz SEE The Three-Cornered Hat

Drewniany ksiaźe SEE The Wooden Prince

Dritte Sinfonie von Gustav Mahler (Gustav Mahler, 1975)
        *Third Symphony; *Third Symphony by Gustav Mahler
    PHA; SIM

Driven Mad by Love SEE Nina

Drobnostki SEE Les petits riens

Drømmebilleder (Hans Christian Lumbye, 1915)
        *Dream Pictures
    ASC (a,i); TER; TES

Drosselbart (Wolfgang Hohensee, 1959)
    REB (a)

Drumming (Steve Reich, 1975)
    MCD (a)

Drums, Dreams and Banjos (Stephen Foster, 1975)
    BAM (a)

Druzhnye serdtsa SEE The Little Stork

The Dryad (Dora Bright, 1908)
    BCB; DAS

The Dryad (Franz Schubert, 1956)
        *Fantasy in F Minor
    TER

La Dryade SEE Eoline

Du-Gul' SEE The Two Roses

Duch Róży SEE Le spectre de la rose

The Duel SEE Le combat

Duet for One SEE Duet for One Person

Duet for One Person (Henry Purcell; Philip Corner; Malcolm
        Goldstein, 1963)
        *Blossoms; *Duet for One
    MCD (a)

Duet with Cat's Scream and Locomotive (1966)
    MCD (a)

Dumbarton Oaks (Igor Stravinsky, 1972)
        *A Little Musical
    BAM (a); REZ (a,b,i); TES

Duo concertant (Igor Stravinsky, 1972)
    BAM (a,i); BAO (a); CLA (i); PHA (i); REZ (a,b,i);
    SIM (i); TES

Dvenadtsat' SEE The Twelve

Dvenadtsat' mesiatsev (Boris Bitov, 1954)
    STO

Dybbuk SEE Dybbuk Variations

Dybbuk Variations (Leonard Bernstein, 1974)
        *Dybbuk
    BAM (a); BAO (a); REZ (a,b!,i); TES

The Dying Swan (Camille Saint-Saëns, 1905)
    *Le cygne; *Den døende svane; *La mort du cygne;
    *Umierajacy labedź; *Umiraĩushchii lebed;
    *Umirajusjtjij lebed
    ASC (a); BAM (a); BAN; BAO (a); BRI; CLA (i); DRE (a);
    PHA; REY (a,i); SIM; TER; TES; TUR (a)

Dziadek do orzechów SEE The Nutcracker

Dziewczyna o szklanych oczach SEE Coppélia

The Eagle (Edward MacDowell, 1929)
    MCD (a)

Early Songs (Richard Strauss, 1970)
    BAM (a); BAO (a); TES

Eaters of Darkness SEE Die im Schatten leben

Ebony Concerto (Igor Stravinsky, 1960)
    BAN; BRI; REZ (b); TES

Eccentrique (Igor Stravinsky, 1972)
    BAM

Echo der Trompeten SEE Ekon av trumpeter

Echoes of Trumpets SEE Ekon av trumpeter

Echoing of Trumpets SEE Ekon av trumpeter

École de danse SEE Scuola di ballo

Ecstasy of Rita Joe (Ann Mortifée, 1971)
    TES

Ecutorial (Edgar Varèse, 1978)
    PHA; SIM

Eden SEE Adam och Eve

Edipe et la Sphinx SEE La rencontre

Egipetskie nochi SEE Cléopâtre

The Egret SEE L'aigrette

Egypta (Walter Meyrowitz, 1910)
    SHE (a,i)

Der eherne Reiter SEE The Bronze Horseman

8 Clear Places (Lucia Dlugoszewski, 1960)
    MCD (a,i)

Eight Jelly Rolls (Jelly Roll Morton, 1971)
    MCD (a,i)

Ekon av trumpeter (Bohuslav Martinů, 1963)
        *Echo der Trompeten; *Echoes of Trumpets; *Echoing
        of Trumpets
    BAM; BAN; BRI; CLA (i); REB (a); TES (i)

Electra (1849)
        *The Lost Pleiad; *La pléiade perdue
    BCB (a)

Electronics (Remi Gassmann; Oskar Sala, 1961)
    BAN; REZ (a,b!,i)

Élégie (Igor Stravinsky, 1945)
    REZ (b)

Les éléments (Johann Sebastian Bach, 1937)
    DET (i)

Les éléments (Giovanni Bajetti, 1847)
        *The Elements
    BCB (a); PHA (a); SIM (a)

The Elements SEE Les éléments (Giovanni Bajetti)

L'elève d'amour SEE Aglaë

Les elfes (Nicolò Gabrielle, 1856)
    BCB (a,i)

Les elfes (Felix Mendelssohn, 1924)
        *The Elves
    BAL; BAN; DET (i); GOO (i,m); TER; TES

Elite Syncopations (Scott Joplin and others, 1974)
    BAM; CLA (i)

The Elves SEE Les elfes (Felix Mendelssohn)

Embattled Garden (Carlos Surinach, 1958)
    PHA; SIM

Embrace Tiger and Return to Mountain (Morton Subotnick, 1968)
    BAM; BRI (i); PHA (i); SIM (i); TES

L'embuscade SEE La prima ballerina

The Emperor Jones (Heitor Villa-Lobos, 1956)
    MCD (a)

Encounter (Wolfgang Amadeus Mozart, 1936)
    REZ (a,b)

Enetime (Georges Delerue, 1963)
        La leçon; *The Lesson; *The Private Lesson
    ASC (a,i); BAM; BAN; TES

L'enfant et les sortilèges (Maurice Ravel, 1925)
        *The Spellbound Child
    BAI (a); BAM; REZ (a,b!,i)

L'enfant prodigue SEE Le fils prodigue

Enigma Variations (Edward Elgar, 1968)
    ASC (a,i); BAM (a,i); BAO (a); BCS (a,i); BRI; CLA;
    TES (i)

Enken i spejlet (Bernard Christensen, 1934)
        *The Widow in the Mirror
    ASC (a); BBP (i)

Ensayo sinfónico (Johannes Brahms, 1951)
    TER

Eoline (Cesare Pugni, 1845)
        *La dryade
    BCB (a,i)

Epic (1957)
    MCD (a)

Epilogue (Gustav Mahler, 1975)
    BAM

Episode fra 1808 SEE Livjaegerne på Amager

An Episode in the Life of an Artist SEE Symphonie fantastique

Episodes (Anton Webern, 1959)
    BAM (a); BAN (i); CLA; PHA (i); REZ (a!,b!,i); SIM (i);
    TER; TES (a)

Epitaph (György Ligeti, 1969)
    BAM

L'épreuve d'amour (Wolfgang Amadeus Mozart, 1936)
        *Chung-Yang and the Mandarin; *Chung-Yang et le
        mandarin cupide; *Die Liebesprobe; *The Proof of
        Love; *The Test of Love
    BCB (a,i); CRB (a); DAS; DET (i); GOO (a,i,m); REG (a);
    ROB (a); TER

Errand Into the Maze (Gian Carlo Menotti, 1947)
    MCD (a)

Errante (Franz Schubert, 1933)
    REZ (a,b,i); TER; TES

Die Erschaffung der Welt SEE La création du monde

Erwachen SEE Despertar

Es mujer (1942)
    MCD (a)

Esik w Ostendzie (Grażyna Bacewicz, 1964)
    TUR (a,i)

La esmeralda (Cesare Pugni, 1844)
    BCB (a,i); CRB (a,i); PHA (a) REB (a); SIM (a); STO (i);
    TER; TES; TUR (a); VER

Esoterik Satie (Erik Satie, 1978)
    PHA; SIM

Esplanade (Johann Sebastian Bach, 1975)
    GRU (a,i)

L'estro armonico (Antonio Vivaldi, 1963)
        *Cycle of Harmony
    BAM; TES

Et Cetera (Paul Martin Palombo, 1973)
    TES

The Eternal Idol (Frédéric Chopin, 1969)
    BAM; BAO; TES

The Eternal Struggle (Robert Schumann, 1940)
    TER; TES

L'étrange farandole SEE Le rouge et noir

Étude (Johann Sebastian Bach, 1926)
    DET (x)

Étude (Knudåge Riisager) SEE Études

Études (Knudåge Riisager after Carl Czerny, 1948)
        *Etude
    ASC (a,i); BAM; BAN; BBP (a,i); CLA (i); PHA; SIM; TES;
    VER

Eugene Onegin (Peter Il'ich Tchaikovsky, 1965)
        *Onegin
    ASC (a); BAM (a); BAO (a); BRI; CLA (i); GRU (a,i); PHA;
    SIM; TES (i)

L'Europa galante (André Campra, 1697)
        *Gallantry in Europe
    PHA (a); SIM (a)

Evening Dialogues (Robert Schumann, 1974)
    BAM; TES

An Evening's Waltzes (Sergei Prokofiev, 1973)
    BAM (a); BAO (a); REZ (a,b,i); TER

Events (Robert Prince, 1961)
    BAN

Every Now and Then (Quincy Jones, 1975)
    BAM

Every Soul is a Circus (Paul Nordoff, 1939)
    CRB

Everyman (Richard Strauss, 1943)
    DAS

Excelsior (Romualdo Marenco, 1881)
    BCB (a,i); PHA (a,i); SIM (a,i)

The Exiles (Arnold Schoenberg, 1950)
    TES

Les exiles célèbres SEE La chaumiére hongroise

Fables for Our Time (Freda Miller, 1947)
    MCD (a)

A fából faragott királyfi SEE The Wooden Prince

Façade (William Walton, 1931)
    *Fasada; *Fassade
    BAM; BAL; BAN; BAO; BCB; BRI; CLA (a,i); CRB (a); DRE
    (a); LAW; PHA; REG (a); REY (a,i); SIM; TER; TES; TUR
    (a)

The Face of Violence SEE Salome (Lester Horton)

Les fâcheux (Pierre Beauchamp, 1661)
    *The Bores
    PHA (a); SIM (a)

Les fâcheux (Georges Auric, 1924)
    *The Bores; *The Intruders
    BRU (i); DET (i); GOO (m); KOC (x); PHA (a); SIM (a)

Facsimile (Leonard Bernstein, 1946)
    BAL; BAM; BAN; LAW; PHA; SIM; TER; TES

Fadetta (Léo Delibes; Jules Massenet; Daniel Auber; Riccardo
    Drigo, 1934)
    TES

Fadette (Gabriel Fauré)
    CRB (a)

The Fair at Sorochinsk (Modeste Moussorgsky, 1943)
    *The Fair at Sorochinsty
    DRE; LAW (i,m); ROB (a); TER

The Fair at Sorochinsty SEE The Fair at Sorochinsk

The Fairies' God-child SEE La filleule des fées

The Fairy and the Knight SEE La Fée et le chevalier

The Fairy Doll SEE Die Puppenfee

The Fairy Queen (Henry Purcell, 1692)
    DAS; PHA (a); SIM (a)

The Fairy's Kiss SEE Le basier de la fée

The Fairy Tale of the Priest and His Workman Balda SEE The
       Tale of the Priest and His Workman Balde

The Fall of a Leaf (Louis Moreau Gottschalk, 1959)
      *The Fall of the Leaf
    MCD (a)

The Fall of the Leaf SEE The Fall of a Leaf

Fall River Legend (Morton Gould, 1948)
    BAL; BAM; BAN; BBT (a,i); CLA (i); CRB; KRO (a);LAW
    (a,i,m); REY (a,i); TER; TES (a,i)

The False Bridegroom (Mikhail Chulaki, 1946)
      *Mnimyĭ zhenikh
    BBP; STO (i)

The False Lord SEE Il finto feudatario

Das Fanal SEE Sklaven

Fancy Free (Leonard Bernstein, 1944)
    BAL; BAM (i); BAN; BAO; BBT (a,i); BRI; CLA (a,i);
    CRB; CRC (a,i); GRU (a,i); KRO (a,i); LAW (i,m); REB

(a); REY (a,i); ROB (a,i); TER; TES (a,i); TUR (a,i);
UNT (i); VER (a,i)

Fanfare (Benjamin Britten, 1953)
BAL; BAM; BAN; DRE (a); REZ (a,b!,i); TER; TES (a)

Fanfarita (Ruperto Chapí y Lorente; zarzuela music adapted
        by Rayburn Wright, 1968)
    TES

Fanga (1949)
    MCD (a)

Fantasia brasileira (Francisco Mignone, 1941)
    REZ (b)

Fantasies (Ralph Vaughan Williams, 1969)
    BAM; REZ (a,b,i); TES

Fantasmi al Grand Hotel (Luciano Chailly, 1960)
        *Ghosts at the Grand Hotel
    PHA; SIM

The Fantastic Toyshop SEE La boutique fantasque

Fantasy (Franz Schubert, 1963)
    REZ (a,b)

Fantasy in F Minor SEE The Dryad (Franz Schubert)

Far from Denmark SEE Fjernt fra Danmark

The Farewell (Gustav Mahler, 1962)
    MCD (a)

Fasada SEE Façade

Fassade SEE Façade

A Faun's Afternoon SEE L'après-midi d'un faune

En fauns eftermiddag SEE L'après-midi d'un faune

Faust (Giacomo Panizza; Michael Costa; Giovanni Bajetti,
    1848)
    BCB (a)

Feast of Ashes (Carlos Surinach, 1962)
    BAM (a); BAN; PHA SIM; TES

La fée aux fleurs SEE Théa

La fée et le chevalier (Gioacchino Rossini; Giovanni Pacini;
    Felice Romani, 1823)
    *The Fairy and the Knight
    PHA (a); SIM (a)

Femina (George W. Byng; Joaquín Valverde, 1910)
    BCB

Les femmes de bonne humeur (Domenico Scarlatti, 1917)
        *Le donne di buon umore; *The Good-Humored Ladies;
        *The Good-Humoured Ladies
    BCB (a,i); BRU (i); CRB; DAS; DET (i); DRE (a); EWE;
    GOO (i,m); KOC (x); LAW (i,m); PHA; SIM

Das Fest in Coqueville (Julius Kalas, 1956)
    REB (a);

Les festes d'Hébé SEE Les fêtes d'Hébé

Le festin (Alexander Borodin, 1911)
    DET (x)

Le festin (Nikolai Rimsky-Korsakov; Mikhail Glinka; Peter
        Il'ich Tchaikovsky; Alexander Glazunov; Modeste
        Moussorgsky, 1909)
    KOC (x)

Le festin de l'araignée (Albert Roussel, 1913)
        *The Spider's Banquet
    BAI (a); BBP (a,i); LAW (m); PHA; SIM

Le festin de Pierre SEE Don Juan (Christoph Willibald von
        Gluck, 1761)

The Festival of Hebe SEE Les fêtes d'Hébé

La fête chez Thérèse (Reynaldo Hahn, 1910)
    BAI (a); BET

La fête étrange (Gabriel Fauré, 1940)
    BAM; BAN; BCS (a,i); BRI; CLA (i); CRB; DAS; DRE (a);
    PHA; SIM

Fête noire (Dmitri Shostakovich, 1971)
    BAM; BAO

Les fêtes chinoises (Jean-Philippe Rameau?, 1751?)
        *Chinese Festival
    PHA (a); SIM (a)

Les fêtes d'Hébé (Jean-Philippe Rameau, 1739)
        *Les festes d'Hébé; *The Festival of Hebe; *Les
        talents lyriques
    PHA (a) SIM (a)

Les fêtes Venitiennes (André Campra, 1710)
        *Venetian Festival
    PHA (a); SIM (a)

Der Feuervogel SEE L'oiseau de feu

Feux rouges, feux verts (Pierre Petit, 1953)
        *Red Lights, Green Lights
    CRB

Fiametta (Léon Minkus, 1863)
        *Plamia liubvi
    BCB (a)

La fiancée du diable (Jean Hubeau, partly after Niccòlo
        Paganini, 1945)
        *The Devil's Bride; *The Devil's Fiancée
    CRB; DAS

Field Figures (Karlheinz Stockhausen, 1970)
    BAM; TES

Field Mass SEE Soldiers' Mass

The Fight between Tancredi and Clorinda SEE Il combattimento
        di Tancredi e Clorinda

Figle szatana (Stanislaw Moniuszko; Adam Münchheimer, 1870)
    TUR (a)

The Figure in the Carpet (George Frederick Handel, 1960)
    BAN; REZ (a,b!,i)

Figure of Memory (Morton Feldman, 1954)
    MCD

La fille aux yeux d'émail SEE Coppélia

La fille de feu SEE Alma

La fille de marbre (Cesare Pugni, 1847)
    *The Marble Maiden
    BCB (a,i); PHA (a,i) SIM (a,i)

La fille du bandit SEE Marco Spada

La fille du Danube (Adolphe Adam, 1836)
    *The Daughter of the Danube
    BCB (a,i); PHA (a,i); SIM (a,i)

La fille du Pharaon SEE The Daughter of Pharaoh

La fille mal gardée (Anonymous music or Louis Hérold or
    Peter Ludwig Hertel, 1786)
    *Córka źle strzezona; *Naughty Lisette; *Den slet
    bevogtede datter; *The Unchaperoned Daughter;
    *Useless Precautions; *Vain Precautions;
    *Vergebliche Vorsicht;   *The Wayward Daughter
    ASC (a,i); BAL; BAM (a,i); BAN (i); BAO (a); BCB (a,i);
    BRI (i); CLA (a,i); CRB; DAC; DOD (a,i); GRU (a,i); KER
    (a,i); KRO (a); LAX (a,i); PHA (a,i); REB (a); REG (a);
    REY (a,i); ROB (a); SIM (a,i); STO (i); TER; TES (i);
    TUR (a); VER

La filleule des fées (Adolphe Adam; Clémenceau de Saint-
    Julien, 1849)
    *The Fairies' God-child
    BCB (i)

Filling Station (Virgil Thomson, 1938)
    BAL; BAM; BAN; BCS (i); CRB; KRO (a,i); LAW (i,m); PHA;
    REZ (a,b!,i); ROB (a); SIM; TER; TES

The Filly (John Colman, 1953)
       *A Stableboy's Dream
    REZ (a,b)

Le fils prodigue (Sergei Prokofiev, 1929)
             *Bludnyĭ syn; *L'enfant prodigue; *Den fortabte
             søn; *The Prodigal Son; *Syn marnotrawny; *Der
             verolene Sohn
    ASC (a,i); BAL (a,i); BAM (i); BAN (a); BAO; BCB; BRI;
    CLA; DRE; GOO (i,m); GRU (a,i); KOC (x); KRO (i); LAX
    (a,i); LAW (a,i,m); PHA; REB (a); REG (a,i); REZ
    (a!,b!,i); ROB (a); SIM; STO (i); TER; TES; TUR (a);
    VER; WIN

La fin du jour (Maurice Ravel, 1979)
    CLA (a,i)

Il finto feudatario (Francesco Antonio de Blasis, 1819)
          *The False Lord
    PHA (a); SIM (a)

Fiorita et la reine des elfrides (Cesare Pugni, 1848)
    BCB (i)

Fire Dance (1895)
          *Flame
    MCD (a)

Fire sidste sange SEE Four Last Songs

Fire temperamenter SEE The Four Temperaments

The Firebird (Igor Stravinsky, 1910) SEE L'oiseau de feu

Firebird (Igor Stravinsky, 1970)
    BAM (a); BAO (a); PHA (i); SIM (i)

First Aerial Station (Louis Spohr, 1976)
    BAM

The Fisherman and his Bride SEE Napoli

Fiskeren og hans brud SEE Napoli

Five Dances (Sergei Rachmaninov, 1975)
    BAM

The Five Gifts (Ernö Dohnányi, 1943)
    DRE; REZ (a,b)

Fjernt fra Danmark (Hans Christian Lumbye; Franz Joseph
        Gläsar; Louis Moreau Gottschalk; Edouard Dupuy;
        Andreas Lincke, 1860)
        *A Costume Ball on Board Ship; *Far from Denmark;
        *Et kostumebal om bord; *Loin du Danemark
    ASC (a,i); BCS; CLA (a,i); PHA (i); SIM (i); TES (i)

Flame SEE Fire Dance

The Flames of Paris (Boris Asaf'ev, 1932)
        *Die Flamme von Paris; *Plamiá parizha; *Plomień
        Paryza; *Triumf respubliki
    BAM; BCB (a,i); PHA (i); REB (a); SIM (i); STO (i);
    TER; TES; TUR (a)

Die Flamme von Paris SEE The Flames of Paris

Die Fledermaus (Johann Strauss, 1958)
    TES

Les fleurs du mal (Claude Debussy, 1970)
        *The Flowers of Evil
    BAM; TES

Flick and Flock SEE Flik e Flok

Flickers (Lionel Nowak, 1941)
    MCD (a)

Flik and Flok SEE Flik e Flok

Flik e Flok (Peter Ludwig Hertel, 1862)
        *Flick and Flock; *Flik and Flok
    BCB; PHA; SIM

Flora and Zephir SEE Flore et Zéphire

Flore et Zéphire (Cesare Bossi, 1796)
        *Flora and Zephir
    PHA (a,i); SIM (a,i)

The Flower Fairy SEE Théa

The Flower Festival at Genzano pas de deux SEE Blomster-
        festen i Genzano

The Flowers of Evil SEE Les fleurs du mal

Fold on Fold SEE Pli selon pli

Folk Dance (Emmanuel Chabrier, 1937)
    REZ (a,b,i)

A Folk Tale SEE Et folkesagn

Et folkesagn (Johan P. Hartmann; Niels V. Gade, 1854)
        *A Folk Tale
    ASC (a,i); BBP (a,i); CLA (i); CRB; TES

Folksay (1942)
    MCD (a)

La folle par amour SEE Nina

La follia di Orlando (Goffredo Petrassi, 1947)
        *Orlando's Madness
    PHA; SIM

Fontaenen i Bakhtjisaraj SEE The Fountain of Bakhchisarai

Fontanna Bachczyseraju SEE The Fountain of Bakhchisarai

The Fool SEE The Buffoon

Fool's Gold SEE L'or des fous

The Footballer SEE Futbolist

For Love or Money (Gilbert Vinter, 1951)
    CRB

For the Sweet Memory of that Day SEE Per la dolce memoria di
    quel giorno

Les forains (Henri Sauguet, 1945)
        *Die Jahrmarktsgaukler; *Strolling Players; *The
        Traveling Players
    BAI (a); BAL; BAM; BAN; BBT (a,i); BRI; CRB; DAS;
    PHA (i); REB (a); SIM (i); TER; TES; VER (a)

Forårets Helliggørelse SEE Le sacre du printemps

Forces of Rhythm (1971)
    BAM (a)

Forevermore (1967)
    MCD (a)

Den förlorade sonen (Hugo Alfvén, 1957)
        *The Prodigal Son; *Der verlorene Sohn
    REB (a)

Den fortabte søn SEE Le fils prodigue

Den forunderlige Mandarin SEE Der wunderbare Mandarin

The Fountain of Bakhchisarai (Boris Asaf'ev, 1934)
        *Bakhchisaraĭskiĭ fontan; *Bakhtjisarajskij
        fontan; *Fontaenen i Bakhtjisaraj; *Fontanna
        Bachczyseraju; *The Fountain of Bakhchisaray; *Der
        Springbrunnen von Bakhtschissarai
    ASC (a); BAM; BAN; BCB (i); BOL (i!); PHA; REB (a); SIM;
    STO; TER; TES; TUR (a)

The Fountain of Bakhchisaray SEE The Fountain of Bakhchisarai

Four Bagatelles (Ludwig van Beethoven, 1974)
    REZ (a,b!,i) TES (i)

Four Last Songs (Richard Strauss, 1970)
        *Fire sidste sange; *Vier letze Lieder
    ASC (a,i); BAM; REZ (a,b,i)

Four Marys (Trude Rittman, 1965)
    BAN; TES

Four Moons (Louis Ballard, 1967)
    TES

Four Schumann Pieces (Robert Schumann, 1975)
    BAM; CLA; PHA; SIM

The Four Seasons (Guiseppe Verdi, 1979)
    PHA; SIM

The Four Seasons (Antonio Vivaldi, 1949)
    BAM; PHA; SIM

The Four Temperaments (Paul Hindemith, 1946)
        *Cztery temperamenty; *Fire temperamenter; *Theme
        and Variations for Piano and Strings; *Die vier
        Temperamente
    ASC (a,i); BAL; BAM; BAN (i); BAO (a); BRI; CLA; DRE
    (a,m); KRO (a); PHA; REB (a); REG (a); REY (a,i); REZ
    (a,b!,i); SIM (i); TER; TES; TUR (a,i)

Les fous d'or (Igor Wakhevitch, 1975)
        *The Golden Fools
    PHA; SIM

The Fox SEE Le renard

Foyer de la danse (Emmanuel Chabrier, 1927)
    BCB

The Frail Quarry SEE Tally-Ho!

Francesca da Rimini (Peter Il'ich Tchaikovsky, 1915)
    BCB (a,i); DRE; GOO (a,i,m); LAW (i,m); PHA; ROB (a);
    SEY (x); SIM; TER; TUR (a,i)

Frankie and Johnny (Jerome Moross, 1938)
    BCS (a,i); CLA; GRU (a,i); TER; TES

Französische Suite (Werner Egk, 1952)
    REG (a)

Frauen unserer Tage (Hans Helmut Hunger, 1960)
    REB (a)

Fräulein Julie SEE Fröken Julie

Freefall (Max Schubel, 1967)
    BRI

Fröken Julie (Ture Rangström, 1950)
        *Fräulein Julie; *Miss Julie; *Panna Julia
    ASC (a,i); BAM; BAN; BBT (a!,i); CRB; PHA; REB (a);
    SIM; TER; TES; TUR (a); VER (a,i)

From 10 to 7 (Lee Haring, after Claudio Monteverdi, 1966)
    MCD (a)

Frontier (Louis Horst, 1935)
        *Perspective No. 1
    MCD (a)

Das Frülingsopfer SEE Le sacre du printemps

Die Frülingsweihe SEE Le sacre du printemps

The Fugitive (Leonard Salzedo, 1944)
    CRB; DAS

Futbolist (Viktor Oransky, 1930)
    PHA; SIM

Gabriella di Vergy (Pietro Romani; Gioacchino Rossini;
        Giacomo Meyerbeer; Paolo Brambilla, 1819)
    PHA (a,i); SIM (a,i)

Gaïane SEE Gayane

Gaîté parisienne (Jacques Offenbach, 1938)
    BAL (i); BAM; BAN; BAO; BCS (a,i); CRB (i); DAS; DET

(i); DOD; DRE (i); EWE; GOO (i,m); KRO (a,i); LAW
(i,m!); ROB (a); SEY (x); TER (i); TES (a)

Gaîté parisienne (Jacques Offenbach, 1978)
    ASC (a); PHA; SIM

Gajane SEE Gayane

Gajaneh SEE Gayane

Gala Performance (Sergei Prokofiev, 1938)
    BAL; BAM; BAN; BAO; BCS (a); CRB; DAS; DRE;
    KRO (a,i); LAW (i,m); ROB (a,i); TER; TES

The Gallant Indies SEE Le Indes galantes

Gallantry in Europe SEE L'Europa galante

The Game Man and the Ladies (Ezra Sims, 1969)
    MCD (a)

Gamelan (Lou Harrison, 1963)
    BRI; TES

Games (1951)
    BAM

Games (Claude Debussy) SEE Jeux

Gartenfest (Wolfgang Amadeus Mozart, 1968)
    BAM; BAO; TES

Gaspard de la nuit (Maurice Ravel, 1975)
    BAM; REZ (a,b!,i)

Gaucho (Emil Reesen, 1931)
    BBP (i)

Der Gaunerstreiche der Courasche (Richard Mohaupt, 1936)
    REB (a); REG (a,i)

Gayane (Aram Khachaturian, 1942)
        *Gaîane; *Gajane; *Gajaneh; *Gayaneh; *Gayne;
        *Happiness
    BCS; DRE (a); LAW (m); PHA; REB (a); REG (a); SIM;
    STO (i); TES; TUR (a)

Gayaneh SEE Gayane

Gayne SEE Gayane

Der Gefangene im Kaukasus SEE The Prisoner of the Caucasus
        (Boris Asaf'ev)

Der Geist der Rose SEE Le spectre de la rose

Gemini (Gustav Mahler, 1972)
    BAM; TES

Gemini (Hans Werner Henze, 1973)
    BAM; TES

Gemma (Nicolò Gabrielli, 1854)
    BCB; PHA (a); SIM (a)

General Colli in Rome SEE Il Generale Colli in Roma

Il Generale Colli in Roma (Ferdinando Pontelibero, 1797)
        *The Ballet of the Pope; *Il Ballo del Papa;
        *General Colli in Rome

PHA (a); SIM (a)

Generation (1968)
    MCD (a)

Genesis (Luigi Nono, 1978)
    PHA; SIM

Die Geschöpfe des Prometheus (Ludwig van Beethoven, 1801)
    *The Creatures of Prometheus; *Die Macht der Musik
    und des Tanzes; *Prometeusz; *Gli uomini di
    Prometeo
    DRE (a); LAW (m); PHA (a,i); REB (a!); REG (a); SIM
    (a,i); TUR (a); WIN

Ghost Town (Richard Rodgers, 1939)
    GOO (i); ROB (a); SEY (x); TER; TES

Ghosts at the Grand Hotel SEE Fantasmi al Grand Hotel

La giara (Alfredo Casella, 1924)
        *Der grosse Krug; *The Jar; *La jarre
    BCB; DRE; PHA (a); REB (a); SIM (a)

Gift of the Magi (Lukas Foss, 1945)
    DAS; TER

The Gingerbread Heart SEE Licitarsko srce

La Gipsy SEE La Gypsy

The Girl with Enamel Eyes SEE Coppélia

Giselle (Adolphe Adam, 1841)
        *Die Wilis; *Les Wilis
    ASC (a,i); BAI (a); BAL (a!,i); BAM (a!,i); BAN (i);

BAO (a!); BCB (a,i); BOL (a,i!); BRI (a,i); CLA (a,i);
CRB (a,i); CRT (a,i!); DAC (a,i!);DAS (a); DET (i); DOD
(i); DRE (a,i,m); EWE; FIS (a,i,m!); GOO (a,i,m); GOU
(i!); GRU (a,i); HEA (a,i); KER (a,i); KOC (x); KRO
(a,i); LAW (a,i,m!); LAX (a,i); PHA (a,i); REB (a,i);
REG (a,i); REY (a,i); ROB (a!,i); ROS (i); SEY (x); SIM
(a,i); STO (i); TER (a); TES (a,i); TUR (a,i); UNT (i);
VER (a); VIV (a,i); WIN

Giselle's Revenge (Adolphe Adam, 1953)
        MCD (a)

La Gitana (Hermann Schmidt; Daniel Auber, 1838)
        *The Gypsy
        BCB (a,i); PHA (a,i); SIM (a,i)

Glagolitic Mass (Leoš Janáček, 1979)
        GRU (a,i)

Glinkaiana SEE Glinkiana

Glinkiana (Mikhail Glinka, 1967)
        *Glinkaiana; *Valse fantaisie
        BAM; REZ (a,b,i); TES

La gloire (Ludwig van Beethoven, 1952)
        BAL; BAN; BBP (a); DRE; REZ (a,b,i); TER

Gloria (Francis Poulenc, 1980)
        CLA

The God and the Bayadere SEE Le dieu et la bayadère

The Gods Amused (Claude Debussy, 1971)
        BAM; TES

The Gods Go A-begging (George Frederick Handel, 1928)
   *Les dieux mendiants
   BCB (a); CRB; DAS; DET (i); EWE; GOO (i); KOC (x); PHA;
   ROS (i); SEY (x); SIM; TER; TES

The Gold Standard SEE Impromptu au bois

The Goldberg Variations (Johann Sebastian Bach, 1971)
   BAM (a!,b); BAO (a!); CLA (i); PHA; REZ (a!,b!,i); SIM;
   TES

The Golden Age (Dmitri Shostakovich, 1930)
   *The Age of Gold; *Zloty wiek; *Zolotoǐ vek
   BCB (i); LAW (m); TES; TUR (a)

The Golden Cockerel SEE Le coq d'or

The Golden Fools SEE Les fous d'or

The Goldfish (Nicholai Tcherepnin, 1937)
   GOO (i,m)

Goluboǐ Dunaǐ (Johann Strauss, 1956)
   STO

The Good-Humored Ladies SEE Les femmes de bonne humeur

The Good-Humoured Ladies SEE Les femmes de bonne humeur

Gorda (David Toradze, 1949)
   STO; TES

Gounod Symphony (Charles Gounod, 1958)
   BAN; REZ (a,b!,i); TES

Goyescas (Enrique Granados, 1940)
  SEY (x)

Gra w karty SEE The Card Party

Graduation Ball (Johann Strauss, 1940)
  ASC (a); BAL; BAM; BAN; BCS (a,i); BRI; CLA (i); CRB;
  DRE (a,i); KRO (a); LAW (i); REY (a,i); ROB (a,i); SEY
  (x); TES; UNT (i); VER

Grand pas classique (Daniel Auber, 1949)
  TES

Grand pas d'action SEE The Sleeping Beauty (Peter Il'ich
  Tchaikovsky)

Grand pas espagnol (Moritz Moszkowski, 1963)
  BAM (a); TES

Grand pas–Glazounov (Alexander Glazunov, 1961)
  TES

Grandstand (1972)
  TES

Graziana (Wolfgang Amadeus Mozart, 1945)
  LAW (i,m); TER; TES

Graziosa (Théodore Labarre, 1861)
  BCB (a)

The Great American Goof (Henry Brant, 1940)
  ROB (a); TER; TES

The Great Detective (Richard Arnell, 1953)
  DRE (m)

The Great Elopement (George Frederick Handel, 1945)
 EWE

El Greco (D. E. Inghelbrecht, 1920)
 BCB (i)

Greek Dreams with Flute (Claude Debussy; Maurice Ohana;
  Edgard Varèse; Alan Hovhaness; Yoritsune Matsu-
  daira; André Jolivet, 1973)
 MCD (a)

The Green Table SEE Der grüne Tisch

Il Gridelino (Filippo d' Agliè, 1653)
  *Ballet du gris de lin; *The Lavender Ballet
 PHA (a); SIM (a)

La grisi (Henri Tomasi, 1935)
 BAI (a)

Det grønne bord SEE Der grüne Tisch

Grosse fuge (Ludwig van Beethoven, 1971)
 BAM

Der grosse Krug SEE La giara

Die grosse Stadt SEE Grossstadt

Grossstadt (Alexandre Tansman, 1932)
  *The Big City; *Die grosse Stadt; *Grossstadt
  1926; *Impressions of a Big City
 BAM (a); BCB (i); DAS; TES

Grossstadt 1926 SEE Grossstadt

Group Accumulation SEE Accumulation, Primary Accumulation,
      Group Accumulation

Der grüne Tisch (Fritz Cohen, 1932)
      *The Green Table; *Det grønne bord; *La table verte;
      *Zielony stol
      ASC (a); BAM; BAN; BCB (a,i); CLA (a,i); DAS; GOO
      (a,i); GRU (a,i); PHA; REB (a); REG (a); REY (a,i);
      SIM; STO (i); TES; TUR (a)

The Guards of Amager SEE Livjaegerne på Amager

The Guests (Marc Blitzstein, 1949)
      BAL; BAM; REZ (a,b!,i); TER; TES

La guiablesse (William Grant Still, 1933)
      BCB

Guignol et Pandore (André Jolivet, 1944)
      BAI (a)

La guirlande de Campra (Georges Auric; Arthur Honegger;
      Daniel-Lesur; Roland-Manuel; Francis Poulenc;
      Henri Sauguet; Germaine Tailleferre, after André
      Campra, 1966)
      BAN; REZ (a,b)

Guns and Castanets (Georges Bizet, 1939)
      BSC (a)

La Gypsy (François Benoist; Ambroise Thomas; Marco Aurelio
      Marliani, 1839)
      *La gipsy; *The Gypsy
      BCB (a,i); PHA (a,i); SIM (a,i)

The Gypsy (François Benoist; Ambroise Thomas; Marco Aurelio
      Marliani) SEE La Gypsy

The Gypsy (Hermann Schmidt; Daniel Auber) SEE La gitana

Gypsy Dances SEE Danses slaves et tziganes

Gyz galasy SEE The Maiden's Tower

H (Krzysztof Penderecki, 1968)
    TUR (a)

H.P. (Carlos Chavez, 1932)
    LAW

Half-time (1969)
    MCD (a)

La halte de cavalerie SEE Cavalry Halt

Hamlet (Boris Blacher, 1950)
    REB (a); REG (a)

Hamlet (Peter Il'ich Tchaikovsky, 1942)
    BAL; BAM; BAN; BBP (a,i); CRB (a); DAS; DRE (a);
    TER; TES (i)

Der Hanschuh (Gerhard Wimberger, 1955)
        *Pas d'illusion
    REG (a,i); WIN

Happiness SEE Gayane

The Happy Coast SEE Coast of Happiness

Harbinger (Sergei Prokofiev, 1967)
    BAM (a); BAO (a); GRU (a,i); TES

Harlequin for President (Domenico Scarlatti, 1936)
REZ (a,b,i)

Harlequin in April (Richard Arnell, 1951)
BAL; BAM; BAN; BBT (a,i); CRB; DRE (m); TER

Harlequinade (Riccardo Drigo, 1965)
BAM (a); BAN; BAO (a); CLA (i); REZ (a,b!,i); TES

Harlequinade pas de deux (Riccardo Drigo, 1952)
REZ (b,i); TES

Harnaschie SEE Harnasie

Harnasie (Karol Szymanowski, 1935)
*Harnaschie
REB (a); STO; TUR (a,i)

The Harvest According (Virgil Thomson, 1952)
BAL; BAN; CRB; TER; TES

Haugtussa (Edvard Grieg Ludt, 1972)
TES

The Haunted Ballroom (Geoffrey Toye, 1934)
BAL; BAM; BAN; BCB; CRB; DAS; DRE; TER; TES

Haus der Schatten (Benjamin Britten, 1955)
REG (a,i)

Haydn Concerto (Franz Joseph Haydn, 1968)
REZ (a,b,i)

Hazaña (Carlos Surinach, 1959)
BRI

Hazard (Leonard Salzedo, 1967)
    BRI

Heads (1973)
    MCD (a)

Hear Ye! Hear Ye! (Aaron Copland, 1934)
    BCB (i); GOO (m)

The Heart of the Hills (Andreĭ Balanchivadze, 1938)
    *The Heart of the Mountains; *Serdᕍse gor
    BCS (i); STO; TES

The Heart of the Mountains SEE The Heart of the Hills

Heiduckenleid SEE Song of the Heiducks

Helen of Troy (Jacques Offenbach, 1942)
    BAL; BAM; BAN; CRB; DRE (a); KRO; LAW (i,m); ROB (a);
    SEY (x); TER; TES

Héliogabale (1976)
    *L'anarchiste couronné; *Heliogabalus
    PHA (i); SIM (i)

Heliogabalus SEE Héliogabale

Here and Now with Watchers (Lucia Dlugoszewski, 1957)
    MCD (a)

Heretic (1929)
    MCD (a)

Las hermanas (Frank Martin, 1963)
    BRI; CLA (i); TES

Hi-kyò (Kazuo Fukushima, 1971)
    BAM

Highland Fling (Stanley Bate, 1947)
    REZ (a,b,i)

Hindu Serenade (1943)
    MCD (a)

Hiob SEE Job

Hip and Straight (Paul Duplessis, 1970)
    TES

L'histoire du soldat (Igor Stravinsky, 1918)
        *L'histoire d'un soldat; *Skazka o beglom soldate
        i cherte; *The Soldier's Story; *The Soldier's Tale
    BAL; BAM; BAN; CRB (a); DRE (a,i); LAW (a,m); PHA (i);
    SIM (i); STO; TES

L'histoire d'un soldat SEE L'histoire du soldat

Die Hochzeit SEE Les noces

Holberg Suite (Edvard Grieg, 1971)
    BAM (a)

The Holy Fair at Bruges SEE Kermessen i Brügge

The Holy Torch (Ernö Dohnányi, 1934)
    BCB

Der holzgeschnitzte Prinz SEE The Wooden Prince

Homage au Ballet (Charles Gounod, 1962)
    TES

Homage to Isadora SEE Brahms Waltzes, Opus 39

Homage to the Queen (Malcolm Arnold, 1953)
    BAM (i); BBT (i); CRB (a); DRE (a); TER (i); TES; VER

Home (Béla Bartók, 1965)
    BRI

Homerische Symphonie (Theodor Berger, 1950)
    REG (a,i)

L'homme et son désir (Darius Milhaud, 1921)
        *Man and His Desire
    BCB (a,i)

Hoop Dance (Ilgenfritz, 1924)
        *Scherzo Waltz
    MCD (a)

Hoopla (1972)
    MCD (a)

L'horloge de Flore SEE Clockwise

Horoscope (Constant Lambert, 1938)
    BCS (a,i); DRE

House (Steve Reich, 1971)
    MCD (a)

A House Divided (Lionel Nowak, 1945)
    MCD (a)

House of Birds (Federico Mompou, 1955)
     DRE (a)

The House Party SEE Les biches

How to Pass, Kick, Fall, and Run (1965)
     MCD (a)

Huddle (1961)
     MCD (a)

Huescape (Pierre Henry; Pierre Schaeffer; Jacques Lasry;
          Bernard Baschet, 1968)
     MCD (a)

The Human Comedy SEE La commedia umana

The Hump-backed Horse SEE The Little Humpbacked Horse
          (Cesare Pugni)

The Hundred Kisses SEE Les cents baisers

The Hungarian Hut SEE La chaumière hongroise

Hungarica (Béla Bartók, 1956)
     DRE

Icare (Serge Lifar, 1935)
          *Icarus
     BAI (a); BCB (i); CRB; GOO (i); PHA (i); SIM (i); TER;
     TES

Icarus (Serge Lifar) SEE Icare

Icarus (Chin-Ichi Matushita, 1964)
    MCD (a); TES

Icarus (Serge Slonimsky, 1971)
    BOL (i!)

The Ice Maiden (Edvard Grieg, 1927)
        *Lediânîâ deva; *Solveig
    BBP; STO (i); TES

Der Idiot (Hans Werner Henze, 1952)
    REG (a,i); WIN

The Idiot (Dmitri Shostakovich, 1979)
    PHA; SIM

Idylle (François Serrette, 1954)
    BBP (a,i); CRB; TES

Igraszka SEE Interplay

Igrouchka (Nikolai Rimsky-Korsakov, 1921)
        *Igroushki; *Russian Dolls; *Russian Toys
    DET (i); GOO (i,m); TER

Igroushki SEE Igrouchka

Ildfuglen SEE L'oiseau de feu

L'île des pirates (Luigi Carlini; Casimir Gide; Gioacchino
        Rossini; Ludwig van Beethoven, 1835)
        *The Isle of Pirates
    SIM (a); PHA (a)

Île des sirènes (Claude Debussy, 1950)
    CRB; DRE

Ilga (Janis Vitolinš, 1937)
    BCS

Illuminations (Benjamin Britten, 1950)
    BAL; BAM; DRE; KRO (i); REZ (a!,b!,i); TER; TES (i)

Die im Schatten leben (Benjamin Britten, 1958)
        *Eaters of Darkness
    TES

Im Zauberladen SEE La boutique fantasque

Images of Love (Peter Tranchell, 1964)
    BAN

Imaginary Film (Arnold Schoenberg, 1970)
    BAM

Imago (Alwin Nikolais; James Seawright, 1963)
    MCD (a,i)

Impressions of a Big City SEE Grossstadt

Impromptu au bois (Jacques Ibert, 1951)
        *The Gold Standard
    DRE

In all Eternity (Antonio Vivaldi, 1972)
    TES

In Nightly Revels (Johann Sebastian Bach, 1973)
    BAM

In scribo Satanis (Otto-Erich Schilling, 1950)
    REG (a,i)

In the Beginning (Peter Sunthorpe, 1969)
    *Adam and Eve
  MCD (a)

In the Night (Frédéric Chopin, 1970)
  BAM (a); BAO (a); REZ (a,b!,i); TES

Incense (Harvey Worthington Loomis, 1906)
  MCD (a)

The Incredible Flutist (Walter Piston, 1938)
  LAW

Incubus (Anton Webern,1962)
  BAM; BAN; TES

Les Indes galantes (Jean-Philippe Rameau, 1735)
    *The Gallant Indies
  BAI (a); BET (a); EWE; PHA (a); SIM (a); TUR (a)

L'indifferent
    *Der Bilderraub
  REG (a)

L'indiscret (Joseph Guy Ropartz, 1943)
  DET (i)

Ines di Castro SEE Doña Ines di Castro

Initials R.B.M.E. (Johannes Brahms, 1972)
  BAM (a); BAO (a)

Insects and Heroes (John Herbert McDowell, 1961)
  MCD (a)

L'insulaire SEE Ozaï

Interludes from "The Fair Pilgrim" SEE La pellegrina

Intermezzo (Johannes Brahms, 1969)
    BAM (a); BAO (a); CLA (i); TES

Les intermittences du coeur (Ludwig van Beethoven, 1974)
        *Vagaries of the Human Heart
    PHA; SIM

Interplay (Morton Gould, 1945)
        *Igraszka
    BAL (i); BAM; BAN (i); BRI; KRO (i); LAW (i,m); REY
    (a,i); REZ (a,b,i); TER; TES (i); TUR (a); VER

Introduction and Allegro for Harp (Maurice Ravel, 1975)
    BAM; REZ (b)

The Intruders SEE Les fâcheux (Georges Auric)

The Invitation (Matyas Seiber, 1960)
    BAM; BAN; BRI; CLA; TES

Iosif prekrasnyĭ SEE Joseph the Beautiful

Iphigenia in Aulis (Christoph Willibald von Gluck, 1905)
    MCD (a)

Irene Holm (Hans Christian Lumbye, 1960)
    ASC (a,i)

Irish Fantasy (Camille Saint-Saëns, 1964)
    BAM; BAN; REZ (a,b,i); TES

Iron Foundry (Alexander V. Mosolov, 1932)
        *Ballet mécanique
    BCB (i); GOO (a,m); LAW

Isadora (Richard Rodney Bennett, 1981)
    CLA (i)

The Isle of Pirates SEE L'île des pirates

Ispytanie damisa SEE Ruses d'amour (Alexander Glazunov)

I͡Unost' SEE Youth

Ivan grosnji SEE Ivan the Terrible

Ivan groznyĭ SEE Ivan the Terrible

Ivan the Terrible (Sergei Prokofiev, 1975)
        *Ivan grosnji; *Ivan groznyĭ
        BAM (a); BOL (i!); CLA (i); PHA (i); SIM (i); TES

Ivesiana (Charles Ives, 1954)
        BAM (a); BAN; KRO (i); REZ (a,b!, i); TER; TES

Ivushka (Orest Evlakhov, 1957)
    STO (i)

Jack in the Box (Erik Satie, 1926)
    DET (x); KOC (x)

Jack Pudding (Hans Werner Henze, 1950)
    WIN

Die Jahreszeiten SEE The Seasons (Alexander Glazunov)

Die Jahrmarktsgaukler SEE Les forains

Jánosík (Václav Kašlík, 1953)
    REB (a)

The Jar SEE La giara

Jardin aux lilas (Ernest Chausson, 1936)
    *Lilac Garden; *Syrenhaven
    ASC (a,i); BAL (i); BAM (a); BAN (i); BAO (a); BCB
    (a,i); BRI; CLA (i); CRB; DAS; DRE (i); GRU (a,i);
    KRO; LAW (i,m); PHA; REY (a,i); REZ (a,b!,i); ROB (a);
    SEY (x); SIM; TER; TES (a); VER

Jardin public (Vladimir Dukelsky, 1934?)
    *Public Garden
    BRU (i); DET (i); GOO (a,m)

Jaroslavna (Boris Tishchenko, 1974)
    PHA; SIM

La jarre SEE La giara

Javotte (Camille Saint-Saëns, 1896)
    BCB; BET; PHA; SIM

Jazz Calendar (Richard Rodney Bennett, 1968)
    TES

Jazz Concert (1960)
    REZ (a,b!,i)

Le jazz hot (Paul Keuter, 1956)
    TES

Jeanne au bûcher (Arthur Honegger, 1939)
    BAI (a)

Jeanne d'Arc SEE Joan of Arc

Jeu de cartes SEE The Card Party

Le jeune homme et la mort (Johann Sebastian Bach, 1946)
        *Den unge mand og døden; *The Young Man and Death
        ASC (a,i); BAL (i); BAM; BAN; BBT (a,i); BRI; CRB; DRE
        (a,i); TER; TES

Jeux (Claude Debussy, 1913)
        *Games; *Spiele
        BAL; BAM (a,i); BAN; BRI; CRB; DRE (a); KOC (x); LAW
        (i,m); PHA (a); REG (a); REZ (a,b,i); SIM (a); TER;
        TES; WIN

Jeux d'enfants (Georges Bizet, 1932)
        *Children's Games
        BAI (a); BCB (i); BRU (i); DRE; GOO (i,m); DET (x); LAW
        (i); REZ (a,b!,i); TER; UNT (i)

Jewels (Gabriel Fauré; Igor Stranvinsky; Peter Il'ich
        Tchaikovsky, 1967)
        BAM (a,i); BAN; BAO (a); BRI; CLA (a,i); GRU (a,i); PHA
        (i); REZ (a,b!,i); SIM (i); TES (a,i)

Jezioro labedzie SEE Swan Lake

Jinx (Benjamin Britten, 1942)
        BAL; BAM; BAN; DRE (a); KRO; PHA; REZ (a,b!,i); SIM;
        TER; TES

Jive (Morton Gould, 1973)
        BAM (a)

Joan of Arc (Nikolai Peiko, 1957)
        *Jeanne d'Arc; *Zhanna d'Ark
        REB (a,i); STO

Joan von Zarissa (Werner Egk, 1940)
        REB (a); REG (a); WIN

Job (Ralph Vaughan Williams, 1931)
        *Hiob
        BAL; BAM; BCB (a,i); CRB (a); DAS; DRE (i,m); FIS
        (a,i,m!); GOO (a,i); REG (a); TER; TES

La jolie fille de Gand (Adolphe Adam, 1842)
        *The Beauty of Ghent
        BCB (a,i); PHA (a); SIM (a)

Jones Beach (Juriaan Andriessen, 1950)
        BAL; BAN; REZ (a,b,i); TER

Joseflegenden SEE Die Josephslegende

Joseph the Beautiful (Sergei Vasilenko, 1925)
        *Iosif prekrasnyǐ
        TES

Die Josephslegende (Richard Strauss, 1914)
        *Joseflegenden; *The Legend of Joseph; *La légende
        de Joseph
        ASC (a); BCB; DRE (m); GOO (m); KOC (x); PHA (i); REB
        (a); REG (a); SIM (i); WIN

Journal (Burt Alcantara, 1971)
        BAM (a); BAO (a)

Journey (Béla Bartók, 1957)
        TER

Jovita (Théodore Labarre, 1853)
        *Les boucaniers
        BCB

The Joys of Winter SEE Les plaisirs de l'hiver

The Judgement of Paris (Cesare Pugni) SEE Le jugement de
        Paris

The Judgement of Paris (Kurt Weill, 1938)
        *Judgment of Paris
        BAM; BAN; CRB; DRE (a); KRO; ROB (a); TER; TES

The Judgment of Paris (Seedo, 1733)
        PHA (a); SIM (a)

Judgment of Paris (Kurt Weill) SEE The Judgement of Paris
        (Kurt Weill)

Le jugement de Paris (Cesare Pugni, 1846)
            *The Judgement of Paris
        BCB (a)

Juice (Meredith Monk; Janet Zalamea; Don Preston, 1969)
        MCD (a)

Juke Box (Alec Wilder, 1941)
        REZ (a,b)

Junction (Johann Sebastian Bach, 1961)
        MCD (a)

Die jungen Damen der Nacht SEE Les demoiselles de la nuit

Jungle (Henk Badings, 1961)
        TES

Junk Dances (1964)
        MCD (a)

Jus primae noctis SEE Das Recht des Herrn

Kaarina, die Königin (Tauno Pulkkänen, 1961)
REB (a)

Des Kaisers neue Kleider SEE Le roi nu

Kaleidoscope (Dmitri Kabalevsky, 1952)
REZ (a,b,i)

Kalevipoeg (Eugen Kapp, 1948)
*Syn Kaleva
STO

Kalkabrino (Léon Minkus, 1891)
BCB; PHA; SIM

Das kalte Herz (Wolfgang Hudy, 1962)
REB (a)

Kameliadamen SEE Kameliendame

Die Kameliendame (Frédéric Chopin, 1978)
*Kameliadamen
ASC (a,i)

Kamennyĭ tsvetok SEE The Stone Flower

Kamienny gość SEE Don Juan (Christoph Willibald von Gluck, 1761)

Kamienny kwiat SEE The Stone Flower

Kammermusik No. 2 (Paul Hindemith, 1978)
CLA (i)

Karnawal SEE Le carnaval

Kartenspiel SEE The Card Party

Kartinki s vystavki SEE Pictures at an Exhibition

Katerina (Anton Rubenstein; Adolphe Adam, 1935)
    BCB

Ein Katzen-Ballet SEE Les demoiselles de la nuit

Kavkazskiĭ plennik (Boris Asaf'ev) SEE The Prisoner of the
    Caucasus (Boris Asaf'ev)

Kavkazskiĭ plennik (Caterino Cavos) SEE Il prigioniero del
    Caucaso

Kermesse in Bruges SEE Kermessen i Brügge

Kermessen i Brügge (Holger Simon Paulli, 1851)
        *The Holy Fair at Bruges; *Kermesse in Bruges;
        *The Three Gifts; *De tre gaver
    ASC (a,i); CLA (i); PHA; SIM; TES

Kettentanz (Johann Strauss; Simon Mayr, 1971)
    BAO (a); TES

Khadra (Jean Sibelius, 1946)
    BAL; BAN; CRB; DRE; TER

Kinderszenen (Robert Schumann, 1974)
        *Scenes of Childhood
    PHA; SIM

Kinetic Molpai (Jess Meeker, 1935)
     MCD (a)

The Kingdom of the Shades SEE La bayadère

The King's Voluntary Corps on Amager SEE Livjaegerne på
          Amager

Die Kirmes von Delft (Hermann Reutter, 1937)
     REB (a); REG (a)

Klatka SEE The Cage

Kleider machen Leute (Karl-Rudi Griesbach, 1954)
     REB (a)

Klementyna (Piotr Perkowski, 1969)
     TUR (a,i)

Klop SEE The Bedbug

The Knight and the Lady SEE Le chevalier et la damoiselle

Knight Errant (Richard Strauss, 1968)
     BRI

Kodaly Dances (Zoltán Kodály, 1971)
     REZ (a,b,i)

Koncert E-moll (Frédéric Chopin, 1937)
     TUR (a)

Konek-gorbunok (Cesare Pugni) SEE The Little Humpbacked
          Horse (Cesare Pugni)

Konek-gorbunok (Rodion K. Shchedrin) SEE The Little Humpbacked
        Horse (Rodion K. Shchedrin)

Des Königs neue Kleider SEE Le roi nu

Konservatoriet (Holger Simon Paulli, 1849)
        *Et Avisfrieri; *The Conservatory; *The Dancing
        School; *A Proposal by Advertising
        ASC (a); BAO (a); BRI (a); CLA; PHA (a,i); SIM (a,i);
        TER; TES (i)

Konstancja SEE Constantia

Kopciuszek SEE Cinderella (Sergei Prokofiev)

La Korrigane (Charles Marie Widor, 1880)
        BCB (a,i); BET

Der Korsar SEE Le corsaire

Korsaren SEE Le corsaire pas de deux

Kortspil SEE The Card Party

Et kostumebal om bord SEE Fjernt fra Danmark

Krasnyĭ mak SEE The Red Poppy

Kreuzbauer Ulrike (Carl-Heinz Dieckmann, 1958)
        REB (a)

Król Wichrów (Feliks Nowowiejski, 1963)
        TUR (a)

Królewski Blazen (Tomasz Kiesewetter, 1958)
    TUR (a)

Ksiezycowy Pierrot SEE Pierrot lunaire

Kurtisanen (Niels Viggo Bentzoon, 1953)
      *The Courtesan
    CRB

Kuruc fairy tale SEE Kuruc mese

Kuruc mese (Zoltán Kodály, 1935)
      *Kuruc Fairy Tale
    BCB

Der Kuss der fee SEE Le basier de la fée

Labyrinth (Franz Schubert, 1941)
    BCS; DRE; LAW (a,i); ROB (a); TER; TES

Labyrinth (Harry Somers, 1968)
    TES

Le lac des cygnes SEE Swan Lake

Die lachende Maske (Wolfgang Hudy, 1964)
    REB (a)

The Ladies of Midnight SEE Les demoiselles de la nuit

Ladies of the Night SEE Les demoiselles de la nuit

The Lady and the Fool (Guiseppe Verdi, 1954)
    BRI; CRB; CRC (a,i); TER; TES (a,i)

The Lady and the Hooligan SEE The Young Lady and the
        Hooligan

The Lady and the Unicorn SEE Der Dame und das Einhorn

Lady from the Sea (Knudåge Riisager, 1960)
    BAM; BAN; TES

Lady into Fox (Arthur Honegger, 1939)
    BCS (a,i); CRB (a); TER; TES

The Lady of Shalott (Jean Sibelius, 1931)
    BCB (i); DAS

The Lady of the Camelias (Guiseppe Verdi, 1951)
    BAL; BAN; CRB; REZ (a,b,i)

Lagertha (Claus Schall, 1801)
    BBP; PHA (a); SIM

Laiderette (Frank Martin, 1954)
    DRE

La laitière suisse SEE Der Schweizer Milchmädchen

Lalla Rookh (Cesare Pugni, 1846)
        *The Rose of Lahore
    BCB (a)

Lament SEE Somnambulism

Lament for Ignacio Sánchez Mejías (Norman Lloyd, 1946)
    MCD (a)

Lament of the Waves (Gérard Masson, 1970)
    BAM

Le langage des fleurs SEE Adélaïde

Lanie SEE Les biches

La lanterne magique SEE Vieux souvenirs

Laudes evangelii (Valentino Bucchi, 1952)
    PHA; SIM

Laurencia (Aleksandr Krein, 1939)
        *Laurensiia
    BCS; PHA; SIM; STO (i); TES

Laurensiia SEE Laurencia

The Lavender Ballet SEE Il gridelino

Leadville (1965)
    MCD (a)

The Leaves are Fading (Antonin Dvořák, 1975)
    BAM (i)

Lebedinoe ozero SEE Swan Lake

Lebedinoje osero SEE Swan Lake

Das Leben eines Wüstlings SEE The Rake's Progress

La leçon SEE Enetime

Lediania deva SEE The Ice Maiden

The Legend of Joseph SEE Die Josephslegende

Legend of Love (Arif Melikov, 1961)
        *Legenda o liubvi; *Legenda o miloŝci; *Legende von
        der Liebe
    BAM; BAN; BOL (i); REB (a,i); STO (i); TES; TUR (a)

The Legend of Ochrid SEE Ohridska legenda

A Legend of Rama (1948)
        CRB

Legenda o liubvi SEE Legend of Love

Legenda o miloŝci SEE Legend of Love

La légende de Cracovie SEE Baŝń krakowska

La légende de Joseph SEE Die Josephslegende

Legende von der Liebe SEE Legend of Love

Leila and Mejnun SEE Leila and Medzhnun

Leila and Medzhnun (Sergei Balasanian, 1947)
        *Leila and Mejnun; * Leili i Medzhnun
    STO (i); TES

Leili i Medzhnun SEE Leila and Medzhnun

Leningrad Symphony (Dmitri Shostakovich, 1961)
        *Leningrader Sinfonie; *Sed'maia simfoniia;

*Shostakovich Seventh Symphony
REB (a,i); STO (i); TES

Leningrader Sinfonie SEE Leningrad Symphony

The Lesson SEE Enetime

Letter to the World (Hunter Johnson, 1940)
CRB; MCD (a); PHA; SIM

Der letzte Schuss (Alexander Karamanov, 1961)
REB (a)

Licitarsko srce (Krĕsimir Baranović, 1924)
*The Gingerbread Heart; *Serce z piernika
DRE; TUR (a)

Die Liebenden von Verona (Leo Spies, 1942)
*The Lovers of Verona
REB (a)

Liebeslieder Walzer (Johannes Brahms, 1960)
BAM (a,i); BAN (a,i); BAO (a); BRI; CLA (i); PHA; REZ
(a,b!,i); SIM; TES

Die Liebesprobe SEE L'épreuve d'amour

Das Liebeswerben auf der Burnt Ranch SEE Rodeo

Das Lied von der Erde (Gustav Mahler, 1965)
*The Song of the Earth
BAM (a!): BAN (a); BRI; CLA; TES (i)

Lieutenant Kije (Sergei Prokofiev, 1963)
*Podporuchik Kizhe
BAM; BAN; PHA; SIM; STO;

Life Guards of Amager SEE Livjaegerne på Amager

The Life Guards on Amager SEE Livjaegerne på Amager

Light (1969–1975)
    MCD (a)

Light trap SEE Piège de luminère

Lilac Garden SEE Jardin aux lilas

The Limpid Brook SEE The Bright Stream

Lis SEE Le Renard

Die listingen Studenten SEE Mischievous Students

The Little Humpbacked Horse (Cesare Pugni, 1864)
        *The Hump-backed Horse; *Konek-gorbunok; *TSar'-
        devitsa
    BAM; BAN; BCB (a); STO; TES

The Little Humpbacked Horse (Rodion K. Shchedrin, 1960)
        *Konek-gorbunok
    PHA; SIM; STO (i)

Little Johnny in Top–Boots (Jenö Kenessey, 1937)
        *Csizmás jankó
    BCB

A Little Musical SEE Dumbarton Oaks

The Little Stork (Dmitrii Klebanov, 1937)
        *Aistenok; *The Baby Stork; *Druzhnye serdtsa;
        *Das Störchlein

BBP (i); REB (a); STO

Livjaegerne på Amager (William Christian Holm, 1871)
        *Episode fra 1808; *The Guards of Amager; *The
        King's Voluntary Corps on Amager; *Life Guards
        of Amager; *The Life Guards on Amager
    ASC (a,i); CLA

Loin du Danemark SEE Fjernt fra Danmark

The Lonely Ones (Zoe Williams, 1946)
    MCD (a)

Lost Illusions (Boris Asaf'ev, 1935)
        *Utrachennye illiuzii
    TES

The Lost Pleiad SEE Electra

Lost Sonata (Igor Stravinsky, 1972)
    REZ (b)

Lot Piece Day/Night (1971)
    MCD

Le loup (Henri Dutilleux, 1953)
        *Ulven; *The Wolf
    ASC (a); BAI (a); BAM; BBT (a,i); BRI; CLA; CRB (i);
    DRE (i,m); TER; TES

Love and the Poet SEE Amor di poeta

The Love of the Three Oranges SEE L'amore delle tre
        melarance

Love the Magician SEE El amor brujo

Love, the Sorcerer SEE El amor brujo

The Lovers of Verona SEE Die Liebenden von Verona

The Loves of Mars and Venus (Symonds; Firbank, 1717)
    BRI (a,i); PHA; SIM

Love's Pupil SEE Aglä̈e

Love's Ruses SEE La toilette de Vénus

Love's Trickery SEE Ruses D'amour

Lucifer (Claude Delvincourt, 1948)
    BAI (a)

Ludas Matyi (Ferenc Szabó, 1960)
        *Matyi Ludas
    REB (a)

Lunar Landing (Jay Miller, 1972)
    MCD (a)

Lyric Suite (Alban Berg, 1953)
    MCD

Lysistrata (Boris Blacher, 1951)
    REB (a); REG (a,i)

Ma mere l'oye (Maurice Ravel, 1912)
        *Mother Goose
    BAI (a); BAM (a); DRE (a); LAW (a,m); PHA; REZ (a,b,i);
    SIM

Maanerenen SEE Mǎnerenen

Die Macht der Musik und des Tanzes SEE Die Geschöpfe des
    Prometheus

Mad Tristan (Richard Wagner, 1944)
    ROB

Madame Chrysanthème (Alan Rawsthorne, 1955)
    BBP (a,i); DRE (a,m); TER

Das Mädchen Hanka SEE Eine Bauernlegende

Das Mädchen mit den Emaille-Augen SEE Coppélia

Das Mädchen und der Rowdy SEE The Young Lady and the
    Hooligan

Mademoiselle Angot SEE Mam'zelle Angot

Mademoiselle Fifi (Theodore Eduard Dufare de Lajart, 1952)
    BAL; BAN; TER

Madrigalesco (Antonio Vivaldi, 1963)
    BAM; TES

Madroños (Moritz Moszkowski; Sebástian Iradier, and others,
    1947)
    BAL; BAN; TER

The Magic Flute (Riccardo Drigo, 1893)
    *Volshebnaia fleĭta
    BCB; PHA; SIM

The Magic Lantern SEE Vieux souvenirs

Magic Swan (Peter Il'ich Tchaikovsky, 1941)
    ROB; SEY (x); TER

The Magnificence of the Universe SEE Dance Symphony

The Magnificent Lovers SEE Les amants magnifiques

The Maid of Cashmere SEE Le dieu et la bayadère

The Maiden's Tower (Afrasiīab Badalbeīli, 1940)
    *Devich'īa bashnīa; *Gyz galasy
    BCS; STO

The Maids (Darius Milhaud, 1957)
    BAM (a); TES

Mala suita (Witold Lutoslawski, 1961)
    TUR (a)

Malédictions et lumières (Gabriel Fauré; Giuseppe Verdi; E.
    Sciortino, 1976)
    *Requiem
    CLA (i); PHA; SIM

La malinche (Norman Lloyd, 1949)
    MCD (a); TES

Mam'zelle Angot (Charles Lecocq, 1943)
    *Mademoiselle Angot
    BBP (a,i); BRI; CLA (i); CRB (a); DRE; KRO; TER

Man and His Desire SEE L'homme et son désir

Der Manager (Hermann Heiss, 1955)
    REG (a)

Il mandarino merariglioso SEE Der wunderbare Mandarin

En måned på landet SEE A Month in the Country

Månerenen (Knudåge Riisager, 1957)
        *Maanerenen; *Månrenen; *Das Mond-Rentier; *Moon
        Reindeer; *Moonreindeer
    ASC (a,i); BAM; BAN; REB (a); TER; TES (i)

Manfred (Peter Il'ich Tchaikovsky, 1979)
    PHA; SIM

Manifestations (Primous Fountain III, 1976)
    BAM

Manon (Jules Massenet, 1974)
    BAM (a); BAO (a); CLA (i); TES

Månrenen SEE Månerenen

Il mantello rosse (Luigi Nono, 1954)
        *Czerwony plaszcz
    TUR (a,i)

The Marble Maiden (Adolphe Adam, 1845)
    BCB (i)

The Marble Maiden (Cesare Pugni) SEE La fille de marbre

La marché des innocents (Cesare Pugni, 1859)
        *A Persian Market; *Parizhskiĭ rynok
    BCB (a,i)

Marche slave (Peter Il'ich Tchaikovsky, 1917)
    MCD (a)

Marco Spada (Daniel Auber, 1857)
        *The Bandit's Daughter; *La fille du bandit

BCB (a,i); PHA (a); SIM (a)

Mardi Gras (Leonard Salzedo, 1946)
        *Shrove Tuesday
    CRB

Marguerite and Armand (Franz Liszt, 1963)
    BAM (a); BAN; GRU (a,i); TES

Le mariage d'Aurore (Peter Il'ich Tchaikovsky, 1922)
        *Aurora's Wedding; *Princess Aurora
    BRU (i); CRB; DET (x); EWE (a); GOO (a,i,m); KOC (x);
    ROB (a!,i); SEY (x); TER

Les mariés de la Tour Eiffel (Georges Auric; Arthur
        Honegger; Darius Milhaud; Francis Poulenc; Germaine
        Tailleferre, 1921)
        *The Wedding Breakfast at the Eiffel Tower
    BCB (a,i); PHA; SIM

Mario and the Magician SEE Mario e il mago

Mario e il mago (Franco Mannino, 1956)
        *Mario and the Magician
    PHA; SIM

La marseillaise (Claude-Joseph Rouget de Lisle, 1915)
        *The Marseillaise
    MCD (a)

The Marseillaise SEE La marseillaise

Marsia SEE Marsyas

Marsyas (Luigi Dallapiccola, 1948)
        *Marsia
    PHA; REG (a,i); SIM; WIN

Marusía Boguslavka (Anatoliĭ Svechnikov, 1951)
    STO

Masekela Language (Hugh Masekela, 1969)
    MCD (a)

Maskarad (Lev Laputin, 1956)
    STO

The Maske of Beauty (1608)
    PHA (a); SIM (a)

A Masque of Beauty and the Shepherd (Christoph Willibald von
        Gluck, 1956)
    TER

Masque of Comus (Henry Purcell or George Frederick Handel,
        1942)
    DAS

The Masquers (Francis Poulenc, 1956)
    REZ (a,b); TER

Mass for Our Time SEE Messe pour le temps présent

Mass for the Present Time SEE Messe pour le temps présent

Le massacre des Amazones (Ivan K. Semenoff, 1951)
    BBT (a,i); PHA; SIM

Les matelots (Georges Auric, 1925)
        *The Sailors
    BCB (i); BRU (i); DET (i); GOO (m); KOC (x); PHA; SIM;
    TER; TES

Matyi Ludas SEE Ludas Matyi

Max und Moritz (Richard Mohaupt, 1949)
     REG (a)

Mayerling (Franz Liszt, 1978)
     CLA (i); PHA; SIM

Mazepa (Tadeusz Szeligowski, 1958)
     TUR (a,i)

Mazurka from "A Life for the Tsar" (Mikhail Glinka, 1950)
     REZ

Meadowlark (Franz Joseph Haydn, 1968)
     BAM; TES

Meat Joy (1964)
     MCD (a)

Medea (Samuel Barber) SEE Cave of the Heart

Medea (Béla Bartók, 1950)
     BAM; BAN; PHA (i); REZ (a,b!,i); SIM; TER (i); TES

Medea and Jason SEE Médée et Jason

Medea i Jazon SEE Médée et Jason

Médée et Jason (Jean-Joseph Rodolphe, 1763)
          *Medea and Jason; *Medea i Jazon
     PHA (a,i); SIM (a,i); TUR

Meditation (Jules Massenet, 1966)
     MCD (a,i)

Meditation (Peter Il'ich Tchaikovsky, 1963)
    BAM; BAN (i); REZ (a,b!,i); TES

Meditation from "Thaïs" (Jules Massenet, 1971)
    BAM

Meditations of Orpheus (Alan Hovhaness, 1964)
    MCD (a)

Medley (1969)
    MCD (a)

Mednyǐ vsadnik SEE The Bronze Horseman

Memory (1972)
    MCD (a)

Mendelssohn Symphony (Felix Mendelssohn, 1971)
    BAM; TES

Las meniñas (Gabriel Fauré, 1916)
        *Les ménines
    DET (x); KOC (x); PHA; SIM

Les ménines SEE Las meniñas

Mercure (Erik Satie, 1924)
        *Mercury
    KOC (x); PHA (a); SIM (a)

Mercury SEE Mercure

The Mermaid (Maurice Ravel, 1934)
    DAS

The Merry Widow (Franz Lehár, 1953)
    *Vilia
  TES

The Merry Wives of Windsor (Valentin Oransky, 1942)
    *Vindzorskie prokaznitsy
  TES

Messe pour le temps présent (Pierre Henry, 1967)
    *Mass for Our Time; *Mass for the Present Time;
    *Msza dzisiejszych czasów
  BAM; TES; TUR (a)

Metallics (Henry Cowell; Henk Badings, 1964)
  MCD (a)

Metamorphoses (Paul Hindemith, 1952)
    *Metamorphosis
  BAL; BAN; DRE (i); REZ (a,b,i); TER; TES

Les metamorphoses (Cesare Pugni, 1850)
  BCB

Metamorphosis SEE Metamorphoses (Paul Hindemith)

Metaphors (Daniel-Lesur, 1965)
  BAM

Metastaseis & Pithoprakta (Iannis Xenakis, 1968)
  REZ (a,b!,i); TES

Metropolitan Daily (Gregory Tucker, 1938)
  MCD (a)

Mevlevi Dervish (Anis Fuleihan, 1929)
  MCD (a)

Midas (Maximilian Steinberg, 1914)
    KOC (x)

The Midnight Sun SEE Le soleil du nuit

A Midsummer Night's Dream (Paolo Giorza) SEE Shakespeare

A Midsummer Night's Dream (Felix Mendelssohn, 1962)
    BAM (a,i); BAN (i); BAO (a); CLA (i); PHA; REZ
    (a,b!,i); SIM; TES (a,i)

Miedziany jeździec SEE The Bronze Horseman

Mignon pas de deux (Ambroise Thomas, 1965)
    TES

The Mikado (Arthur Sullivan, 1954)
    TER

The Mind is a Muscle, Part I SEE Trio A

Les mines de Syracuse SEE Rosida

The Minotaur (Elliott Carter, 1947)
    REZ (a,b,i)

Miracle in the Gorbals (Arthur Bliss, 1944)
    BBP (a,i); CRB; DAS; DRE (a); TER

The Miraculous Mandarin SEE Der wunderbare Mandarin

Les mirages (Henri Sauguet, 1947)
    BAI (a); BBP (i); CRB; PHA; SIM; TER; TES

Mirandolina (Sergei Vasilenko, 1949)
        STO

Mirror (Lars-Erik Larssen, 1957)
        DRE

A Mirror for Witches (Denis ApIvor, 1952)
        BAL; BAN; BBT (a,i); CRB; DRE

Misalliance (Jacques Ibert, 1972)
        MCD (a)

Mischievous Students (Ferenc Farkas, 1949)
        *Die listingen Studenten
        REB (a)

Miss Julie SEE Fröken Julie

Missa Brevis (Zoltán Kodály, 1958)
        TES

Mnimyĭ zhenikh SEE The False Bridegroom

Modern Jass: Variants (Gunther Schuller, 1960)
        BAN; REZ (a,b!,i)

Mods and Rockers (The Beatles, 1963)
        BRI

Der Mohr von Venedig (Boris Blacher, 1955)
        *The Moor of Venice
        REB (a); REG (a,i)

Le Molière imaginaire (Rinaldi Rota, 1976)
        PHA (a); SIM (a);

Moments (Anton Webern, 1968)
    BRI

Momentum (Peter Il'ich Tchaidovsky, 1969)
    BAM

Das Mond-Rentier SEE Månerenen

Monkshood's Farewell (1974)
    MCD (a)

Monotones 1 and 2 (Erik Satie, 1965)
    BAM; BAM; BRI; CLA (i); TES

Monotony SEE Somnambulism

A Month in the Country (Frédéric Chopin, 1976)
        *En måned på landet
    ASC (a); BAM (a,i); CLA (i); GRU (a,i); PHA; SIM

Monument voor een gestorven jongen (Jan Boerman, 1965)
        *Monument for a Dead Boy
    BAM (a); BAO (a); TES (i)

Monument for a Dead Boy SEE Monument voor een gestorven
    jongen

Monumentum pro Gesualdo (Igor Stravinsky, after Carlo
    Gesualdo, 1960)
        *Movements
    BAM (a); REZ (a,b!,i) TES

Moon Reindeer SEE Månerenen

Moonreindeer SEE Månerenen

The Moor of Venice SEE Der Mohr von Venedig

The Moorish Woman in Spain SEE Zoraiya

The Moor's Pavane (Henry Purcell, 1949)
        *Morens pavane
        ASC (a,i); BAM (a); BAO (a); CLA (i); GRU (a,i); MCD
        (a,i); PHA (i); REY (a,i); SIM (i); TES

Morens pavane SEE The Moor's Pavane

La mort du cygne SEE The Dying Swan

La morte di Cleopatra (Gasparo Angiolini, 1780)
        *The Death of Cleopatra
        PHA (a); SIM (a)

Mother Goose SEE Ma mère l'oye

Mother Goose Suite (Maurice Ravel, 1943)
        BAL; BAM; BAN; KRO; REZ (a,b!); TER; TES

Mourning Orders in 24 Hours SEE Deuil en 24 heures

Movements (Igor Stravinsky, 1960) SEE Monumentum pro
        Gesualdo

Movements (Igor Stravinsky, 1963) SEE Movements for Piano and
        Orchestra

Movements for Piano and Orchestra (Igor Stravinsky, 1963)
        *Movements
        BAM (a); BAN; REZ (a,b!,i); TES

Moves (1959)
    BAM; BAN; PHA; SIM; TES

Moyen age (Girolamo Frescobaldi, 1926)
    MCD (a)

Mozart Concerto (Wolfgang Amadeus Mozart, 1966)
       *Concerto for Flute and Harp
    BAM; TES

Mozartiana (Peter Il'ich Tchaikovsky, 1933)
    CLA (i); LAW (i,m); REZ (a,b,i); TER; TES

Mr. Punch (Arthur Oldham, 1946)
    DAS

Mr. Puppet (1947)
    MCD (a)

Msza dzisiejszych czasow SEE Messe pour le temps présent

Musical Chairs SEE Commedia balletica

Mutations (Karlheinz Stockhausen, 1970)
    BAM (a); BAO (a); PHA; SIM; TES

The Mute Wife (Niccolò Paganini, 1944)
    TER; TES

Mythical Hunters (Oedoen Partos, 1965)
    MCD (a); TES (i)

N.Y. Export, Op. Jazz (Robert Prince, 1958)
       *New York Export, Op. Jazz
    BAM (a); BAN; TER (i); TES

Na kwaterze (Stanislaw Moniuszko, 1868)
TUR (a)

Der Nachmittag eines Fauns SEE L'après-midi d'un faune

Die Nachtigall (Otto Reinhold, 1958)
*The Nightingale
REB (a)

Der nackte König SEE Le roi nu

Nad pieknym Dunajem SEE Le beau Danube

Nagi Kziaze (Romauld Twardowski, 1964)
TUR (a)

The Naiad SEE Ondine (Cesare Pugni)

The Naiad and the Fisherman SEE Ondine (Cesare Pugni)

Namouna (Édouard Lalo, 1882)
BCB (a,i); BET; DRE (a,m); LAW (m); PHA; SIM

Napoli (Holger Simon Paulli; Edvard Helsted; Niels V. Gade;
Hans Christian Lumbye, 1842)
*The Fisherman and his Bride; *Fiskeren og hans
brud; *Neapol; *Rybak i jego narzeczona
ASC (a,i); BAL; BAM (a); BAN; BAO (a); BCS (i); BRI
(i); CLA (i); CRB (a); DOD (i); GRU (a,i); PHA (a,i);
SIM (a,i); TER (a); TES (i); TUR (a); VER

Narcisse (Nikolai Tcherepnin, 1911)
*Narcissus
DET (i); GOO (m); KOC (x); PHA; SIM

Narcissus (Robert Prince) SEE Narkissos

Narcissus (Nikolai Tcherepnin) SEE Narcisse

Narcissus Rising (1968)
     MCD (a)

Narkissos (Robert Prince, 1966)
          *Narcissus
     BAN; REZ (a,b)

Der Narr SEE The Buffoon

Nathalie SEE Der Schweizer Milchmädchen

Native Dancers (Vittorio Rieti, 1959)
     REZ (a,b!)

Naughty Lisette SEE La fille mal gardée

Nautch (1908)
     MCD (a)

Nautéos (Jeanne Leleu, 1947)
     BBP (i); CRB (i)

Neapol SEE Napoli

Negro Spirituals (1928-1942)
     MCD (a)

Nestinarka (Marin Goleminov, 1942)
     REB (a)

Neue Odyssee (Viktor Bruns, 1957)
          *Nowa Odyseja
     REB (a); TUR (a)

Neuvième symphonie (Ludwig van Beethoven, 1964)
    *The Ninth Symphony
    PHA (i); SIM (i)

New Dance (Wallingford Riegger, 1935)
    MCD (a,i)

A New Lord Comes SEE La somnambule (Louis Hérold)

New York Export, Op. Jazz SEE N.Y. Export, Op. Jazz

The New Yorker (George Gershwin, 1940)
    BCS; SEY (x)

Night (Luciano Berio, 1966)
    BAN

The Night and Silence (Johann Sebastian Bach, 1958)
    BRI

Night City (Béla Bartók, 1961)
    *Nochnoĭ gorod
    TES

Night Journey (William Schuman, 1947)
    CRB

Night on Bald Mountain SEE La nuit sur le Mont Chauve

Night Shadow (Vittorio Rieti, after Vincenzo Bellini, 1946)
    *La sonnambula; *La somnambule; *Søvngaengersken
    ASC (a); BAL; BAM (a); BAN; BBT (a,i); BRI; CLA; CRB;
    PHA (i); REZ (a,b!,i); SEY (x); SIM (i); TER; TES; VER

Night Song (Alan Hovhaness, 1967)
    TES

The Nightingale (Mikhail Kroshner, 1939)
        *Soloveĭ
    BCS; STO

The Nightingale (Otto Reinhold) SEE Die Nachtigall

The Nightingale (Igor Stravinsky) SEE Le chant du rossignol

The Nightingale and the Rose SEE Le rossignol et la rose

Nightwandering (Bo Nilsson, 1958)
    MCD (a)

Nightwings (John LaMontaine, 1966)
    BAM; TES

Nijinski, clown de Dieu SEE Nijinsky, clown de Dieu

Nijinsky, clown de Dieu (Pierre Henry; Peter Il'ich
        Tchaikovsky, 1971)
        *Nijinski, clown de Dieu; *Nijinksy, Clown of God
    BAM (a,i); BAO (a); PHA (i); SIM (i); TES

Nijinksy, Clown of God SEE Nijinsky, clown de Dieu

Nimfa Diany SEE Sylvia

Nina (Louis Persius, 1813)
        *Driven Mad by Love; *La folle par amour
    BCB (a); PHA; SIM

The Ninth Symphony SEE Neuvième symphonie

Niobe (Juliusz Luciuk, 1967)
    TUR (a)

Nobilissima visione (Paul Hindemith, 1938)
        *Noble Vision; *Saint Francis; *St. Francis
    BCS (a,i); CRB; DET (i); DRE (a); GOO (i,m); LAW
    (a,i,m); PHA; REB (a); REG (a); ROB (a); SEY (x); SIM;
    TER; TES; WIN

Noble Vision SEE Nobilissima visione

Il noce di Benevento (Franz Xavier Süssmayr, 1812)
        *The Walnut Tree of Benevento
    PHA (a,i); SIM (a,i)

Les noces (Igor Stravinsky, 1923)
        *Bryllupet; *Die Hochzeit; *Svadebka; *The
        Wedding; *Wesele
    ASC (a); BAL; BAM (a); BAN; BAO (a); BCB (a,i); BRI;
    BRU (i); CLA (i); CRB; GOO (a,m); KOC (x); LAW (a,m);
    PHA; REB (a); ROB (a); SIM; TER; TES (a,i); TUR (a); WIN

Noch' i den' SEE La nuit et le jour

Noch' pered rozhdestvom SEE Christmas Eve

Nochnoĭ gorod SEE Night City

Noctambules (Humphrey Searle, 1956)
    DRE; TER

Nocturne (Frederick Delius, 1936)
    BCB; CRB (a); DAS: DRE

Nocturne (Jean-Philippe Rameau, 1933)
    GOO

Nøddeknaekkeren SEE The Nutcracker

Noir et blanc SEE Suite en blanc

Nomus alpha (Iannis Xenakis, 1969)
    BAM; PHA; SIM; TES

Nostalgia (Burt Alcantara; Jennifer Muller, 1971)
    MCD (a)

Notebook (1968)
    MCD

Notre Dame de Paris (Maurice Jarre, 1965)
    PHA; SIM

Notre Faust (Johann Sebastian Bach; Léon Minkus; Harry
        Warren, 1975)
    GRU (a,i); PHA (a,i); SIM (a)

Notturno Montmartre (Hermann Reutter, 1952)
    REG (a)

Nowa Odyseja SEE Neue Odyssee

Le nozze degli dei (Giovanni Carlo Coppola?, 1637)
        *The Wedding of the Gods
    PHA (a); SIM (a)

La nuit (Henri Sauguet, 1949)
    BBT (a)

Une nuit d' Egypte SEE Cléopâtre

La nuit de Saint—Joan (Hugo Alfvén, 1920)
    BCB

La nuit et le jour (Léon Minkus, 1883)
    *Noch' i den'
    BCB

La nuit sur le Mont Chauve (Modeste Moussorgsky, 1946)
    *Night on Bald Mountain
    DET (x)

Der Nussknacker SEE The Nutcracker

The Nutcracker (Peter Il'ich Tchaikovsky, 1892)
    *Casse-noisette; *Dziadek do orzechów;
    *Nøddeknaekkeren; *Der Nussknacker; *Shchelkunchik;
    *Sjtjelkuntjik
    ASC (a,i); BAI (a); BAL (a); BAM (a,i); BAN (i); BAO
    (a); BCB (a); BOL (a,i!); BRI (a); CLA (i); CRB; CRC
    (a,i); DAC (a,i!); DAS; DET (i); DOD (a,i); DRE (a,i,m);
    EWE (a); FIS (a,i,m!); GOU (i); GRU (a,i); KER (i); KRO;
    LAW (a,i,m); LAX (a,i!); MAY (a!,i); PHA (a,i); REB (a);
    REG (a); REY (a,i) REZ (a!,b!,i); ROS (i); SEY (x); SIM
    (a,i); STO (i); TER; TES (a,i); TUR (a,i); UNT (i); VER
    (a,i); VIV (a,i); WIN

The Nymph of Diana SEE Sylvia

La nymphe de Diane SEE Sylvia

Die Nymphe der Diana SEE Sylvia

O Rose, Thou Art Sick SEE La rose malade

Obbligato '69 N.Y. (1969)
    MCD (a)

Ochridische legende SEE Ohridska legenda

Ochrydzka legenda SEE Ohridska legenda

Octandre (Edgar Varèse, 1971)
    REZ (a,b)

Octavius in Egypt SEE Ottaviano in Egitto

Octet (Igor Stravinsky, 1958)
    REZ (b); TER

October Parade (1971)
    MCD (a)

Octuor (Igor Stravinsky, 1972)
    BAM; REZ (a,b)

Oczekiwanie (Augustin Bloch, 1964)
    TUR (a,i)

Ode (Nicolas Nabokov, 1928)
    KOC (x)

Ode (Igor Stravinsky, 1972)
    BAM; PHA; REZ (a,b); SIM

L'oeuf à la coque (Maurice Thiriet, 1948)
        *The Boiled Egg; *The Soft-Boiled Egg
    BAL; BAN; BBT (i); CRB; TER

Of Love and Death SEE Del amor y de la muerte

Offenbach in the Underworld (Jacques Offenbach, 1955)
    BAM; BBP (i); TER

Offering to Liberty SEE Offrande à la liberté

Offrande à la liberté (Claude-Joseph Rouget de Lisle,
      1792)
      *Offering to Liberty
    PHA; SIM;

Offrande choreographique (Johann Sebastian Bach, 1971)
      *Choreographic Offering
    BAM (a); PHA; SIM;

Ognisty ptak SEE L'oiseau de feu

Ohridska legenda (Stevan Hristić, 1947)
      *The Legend of Ochrid; *Ochridische   Legende;
      *Ochrydzka legenda
    CRB; REB (a); TUR (a)

L'oiseau de feu (Igor Stravinsky, 1910)
      *Der Feuervogel; *The Firebird; *Ildfuglen;
      *Ognisty ptak; *Shar ptiza; *Zhar-ptitsa
    ASC (a,i); BAI (a); BAL (a,i); BAM (a); BAN (i); BAO
    (a); BCB (a); BRI; BRU (i); CLA (a,i); CRB (i); CRC
    (a,i); DAS; DET (i); DOD (a,i); DRE (a,i,m); FIS (a,m!);
    GOO (a,i,m); GRU (a,i); KOC (x); KRO (a,i); LAW (a,i,m);
    LAX (a,i); PHA (a); REB (a); REG (a); REY (a,i); REZ
    (a!,b!,i); ROS (i); SIM (a); STO (i); TER; TES (a,i);
    TUR (a,i); UNT (i); VER (i); VIV (a,i); WIN

Old King Cole (Ralph Vaughan Williams, 1923)
      DRE

Old Memories SEE Vieux souvenirs

Olympics (Toshiro Mayuzumi, 1966)
      BAM; BAN (i); TES

L'ombra della fidanzata SEE Il prigioniero del Caucaso

L'ombre (L. Wilhelm Maurer, 1839)
        *Pas de l'ombre; *The Shade
    BCB (a,i); PHA; SIM

On Stage! (Norman Dello Joio, 1945)
    CRB; DAS; LAW (a,i,m); TER; TES

On the Brink of Time (Morton Subotnick, 1969)
    MCD (a)

Once More, Frank (Carson C. Parks; Harold Arlen; Johnny
        Mercer; Dean Kay; Kelly Gordon, 1976)
    BAM

Once Upon a Time (Johannes Brahms; Sergei Prokofiev; Claude
        Debussy; Domenico Scarlatti, 1951)
    MCD (a)

Ondine (Hans Werner Henze) SEE Undine (Hans Werner Henze)

Ondine (Cesare Pugni, 1843)
        *The Naiad; *The Naiad and the Fisherman; *Undine
    BCB (a,i); HEA (a!,i); UNT (i)

Ondine (Antonio Vivaldi, 1949)
    REZ (a,b)

Ondyna SEE Undine (Hans Werner Henze)

The One Hundreds (1970)
    MCD (a)

One Two Three (Ben-Zion Orgad, 1968)
    BRI; MCD (a)

Onegin SEE Eugene Onegin

Oneness SEE Orrenda

Ontogeny (Karel Husa, 1971)
    BAM

Opus I (Anton Webern, 1965)
    BAM; TES

Opus 12 (Béla Bartók, 1964)
    TES

Opus 34 (Arnold Schoenberg, 1954)
    BAN; REZ (a,b,i); TER

Opus 51 (Vivian Fine, 1938)
    MCD (a)

Opus 65 (Teo Macero, 1965)
    TES

Opus Lemaître (Johann Sebastian Bach, 1973)
    BAM; TES

L'or des fous (Girolamo Arrigo, 1975)
        *Fool's Gold
    PHA (i); SIM (i)

Orbs (Ludwig van Beethoven, 1966)
    MCD (a,i)

Orfeǐ SEE Orpheus

Orfeusz SEE Orpheus

Oriane et le prince d'amour (Florent Schmitt, 1938)
    *Oriane la sans-eagle
  BCS (i); CRB

Oriane la sans-eagle SEE Oriane et le prince d'amour

Orient–Occident (Iannis Xenakis, 1975)
  PHA; SIM

Les orientales (Alexander Glazunov; Christian Sinding; Anton
    Arensky; Edvard Grieg; Alexander Borodin, 1910)
    *The Orientals
  KOC (x); PHA; SIM

The Orientals SEE Les orientales

The Origin of Design (George Frederick Handel, 1932)
  EWE

Orlando's Madness SEE La follia di Orlando

The Orphan of China SEE L'orphelin de la Chine

L'orphelin de la Chine (Christoph Willibald von Gluck, 1774)
    *The Orphan of China
  PHA (a,i); SIM (a,i)

Orpheus (Igor Stravinsky, 1948)
    *Orfeï; *Orfeusz
  BAL (a,i); BAM; BAN (a); BAO; BBT (a,i); CLA (i); CRB
  (a); GRU (a,i); KRO; LAW (a,i,m); PHA; REB (a); REG
  (a,i); REZ (a,b!,i); SIM; STO; TER (a); TES (a); TUR (a)

Orpheus and Eurydice (Christoph Willibald von Gluck, 1941)
  DAS; ROB (a)

Orrenda (Cara Bradbury Marcus, 1969)
    *Oneness
  MCD (a)

Otello (1818)
    *Othello
  BCB (a,i); PHA (a); SIM (a)

Otello (Aleksei Machavriani, 1957)
  STO (i); TUR (a,i)

Othello (1818) SEE Otello (1818)

Othello (Jan Hanuš, 1959)
  REB (a)

Other Dances (Frédéric Chopin, 1976)
  BAM

Ottaviano in Egitto (Giacomo Panizza, 1829)
    *Octavius in Egypt
  PHA (a); SIM (a)

Out of Lesbos (James Clouser, 1966)
  TES

The Ox on the Roof SEE Le boeuf sur le toit

Ozaï (Casimir Gide, 1847)
    *L'insulaire
  BCB (a,i)

Padmâvatî (Albert Roussel, 1923)
  BET (a)

Paean (Ernest Chausson, 1957)
    TER (i)

Pafio e Mirra (Antonio Salieri, 1778)
        *Pafius and Mirra
    PHA (a); SIM (a)

Pafius and Mirra SEE Pafio e Mirra

Paganini (Sergei Rachmaninov, 1939)
    BAM (a); BAN; BCS (a,i); CRB; DRE; GOO (m); LAW (i,m);
    PHA; ROB (a); SEY (x); SIM; STO; TER; TES

The Pages of the Duke de Vendôme SEE Le pages du Duc de
        Vendôme

Les pages du Duc de Vendôme (Adalbert Gyrowetz, 1815)
        *The Pages of the Duke de Vendôme
    BCB (a)

Le palais de cristal (Georges Bizet, 1947)
        *Le palais de crystal; *Symphony in C
    ASC (a,i); BAI (a); BAL; BAM (a); BAN; BAO (a); CLA;
    DRE (a); KRO; LAW (i,m); PHA; REZ (a,b!i); SIM; TER;
    TES; VER

Le palais de crystal SEE Le palais de cristal

PAMTGG (Roger Kellaway, after Stan Applebaum and Sid
        Woloshin, 1971)
    REZ (a,b,i)

Pan Twardowski (Ludomir Rozycki, 1921)
    REB (a); TUR (a,i)

Panamerica (1960)
    REZ (a,b!i)

Pancernik Potiomkin (Juliusz Luciuk, 1967)
TUR (a)

Pandora (Roberto Gerhard, 1944)
DAS

Panna Julia SEE Fröken Julie

Le papillon (Jacques Offenbach, 1860)
*The Butterfly
BCB (a,i); PHA (a,i); SIM (a,i)

Les papillons (Robert Schumann, 1912)
DET (x); GOO (i,m); KOC (x)

Les papillons (Leopold Wenzel, 1901)
BCB (i)

Paquerette (François Benoist, 1851)
BCB (a)

Paquita (Édouard Deldevez, 1846)
BCB (a,i); CLA; TER; TES

Paquita (Léon Minkus, 1964)
BAM (a)

Paquita pas de deux (Léon Minkus, 1957)
TES

Parade (Erik Satie, 1917)
ASC (a); BAI (a); BAM (a); BAO (a); BCB (a); CLA (i);
DRE (a,m); GRU (a,i); KOC (x); LAW; PHA (a,i); SIM
(a,i); TES

Parades and Changes (Morton Subotnick, 1967)
MCD (a)

Paradise Lost (Marius Constant, 1967)
BAM; BAN (i); PHA; SIM; TES

Parisiana (Germaine Tailleferre, 1953)
CRB

Parizhskiĭ rynok SEE La marché des innocents

Part Real-Part Dream (Mordecai Seter, 1965)
MCD (a)

Partisan Days (Boris Asaf'ev, 1937)
*Partizanskie dni
STO

Partizanskie dni SEE Partisan Days

Pas d'acier (Sergei Prokoviev, 1927)
*Dance of Steel; *Der stählerne Schritt; *Stal'noĭ
skok; *Stalowy krok; *The Steel Trot
KOC (x); LAW (m); PHA; REB (a); SIM; TUR (a)

Pas d'illusion SEE Der Hanschuh

Pas de deux (Peter Il'ich Tchaikovsky) SEE Tchaikovsky pas
de deux

Pas de deux af Blomsterfesten i Genzano SEE Blomsterfesten i
Genzano

Pas de deux af Korsaren SEE Le corsaire pas de deux

Pas de Deux and Divertissement (Léo Delibes, 1965)
    BAN; REZ (a,b,i)

Pas de deux romantique (Carl Maria von Weber, 1950)
    REZ (a,b)

Pas de dix (Alexander Glazunov, 1955)
    BAM; BAN; REY (a,i); REZ (a,b,i); TER; TES

Pas de Duke (Duke Ellington, 1976)
    BAM

Pas de l'ombre SEE L'ombre

Pas de quatre (Cesare Pugni, 1845)
    ASC (a,i); BAL (a!,i); BAM (a!,i); BAN (a,i); BAO (a!);
    BCB (a,i); LAW (m); MAY (a!,i); PHA (a); REG (a); REY
    (a,i); ROB (a,i); SIM (a); TER (a); TES (a); TUR (a);
    VER (a)

Pas de trois (Mikhail Glinka, 1955)
         *Pas de trois II
    REZ (a,b); TER; TES

Pas de trois (Léon Minkus, 1951)
    REZ (a,b,i); TER; TES

Pas de trois II SEE Pas de trois (Mikhail Glinka)

Pas des déesses (John Field, 1954)
    BAM; BAN (i); BRI; CLA (i); TER; TES

Passacaglia and Fugue in C Minor (Johann Sebastian Bach,
         1938)
         *Passacaglia in C Minor
    MCD (a)

Passacaglia in C Minor SEE Passacaglia and Fugue in C Minor

Passin' Through (1959)
  MCD (a)

La pastorale (Georges Auric, 1926)
  DET (i); KOC (x)

Pastorale (Wolfgang Amadeus Mozart, 1950)
  DRE

Pastorale (Leo Spies, 1942)
  REB (a)

Pastorale (Charles Turner, 1957)
  REZ (a,b,i); TER

Pastorela (Paul Bowles, 1941)
  BCS (a,i); REZ (a,b,i)

The Path of Thunder (Kara Karaev, 1957)
        *Sklakiem gromu; *Tropoíu groma
  STO (i); TES; TUR (a)

Les patineurs (Giacomo Meyerbeer, 1937)
        *The Skaters
  BAL; BAN; BAM; BCB (i); BRI; CLA (i); CRB (a); CRT
  (a,i); DRE; GRU (a,i); LAX (a,i); REY (a,i); TER; TES

Les patineurs (Cesare Pugni) SEE Les plaisirs de l'hiver

Pavane (Maurice Ravel, 1975)
  BAM; REZ (a,b)

The Pavilion SEE Le pavillon

Le pavillon (Alexander Borodin, 1936)
        *The Pavilion
    GOO (i,m)

Le pavillon d'Armide (Nikolai Tcherepnin, 1907)
        *Armida's Pavilion; *Pavil'on Armidy
    BCB (a); CRB; DAS; DET (i); GOO (m); KOC (x); PHA; SIM;
    STO

Pavil'on Armidy SEE Le pavillon d'Armide

Paw i Dziewczyna (Tadeusz Szeligowski, 1949)
    TUR (a)

Pelican (1963)
    MCD (a)

Pelléas and Mélisande SEE Pelléas et Mélisande (Arnold
        Schoenberg)

Pelléas et Mélisande (Gabriel Fauré, 1953)
    BBP

Pelléas et Mélisande (Arnold Schoenberg, 1969)
        *Pelléas and Mélisande
    BAM

La pellegrina (Luca Marenzio; Emilio de Cavaliere; Jacopo
        Peri; Guilio Caccini; Cristofano Malvezzi;
        Antonio Archilei; Giovanni Bardi, 1589)
        *Interludes from "The Fair Pilgrim"
    PHA (a,i); SIM (a,i)

Per la dolce memoria del quel giorno (Luciano Berio, 1974)
        *For the Sweet Memory of that Day; *I trionfli di
        Petrarca; *The Triumphs of Petrarch
    PHA (i); SIM (i)

Percussion for Six-men (Lee Gurst, 1969)
    TES

Percussion for Six-women (Lee Gurst, 1971)
    TES

Perhaps To-morrow! (Jenö Kenessey, 1937)
    BCB (i)

La péri (Friedrich Bürgmuller, 1843)
    BAM; BAN; BCB (a,i); LAW (m); PHA (a,i); SIM (a,i)

La péri (Paul Dukas, 1912)
    BAI (a); CRC (a,i); DRE (a,i,m); PHA; SIM; TER; TES

The Perils of Everybody SEE The Concert

Persée (Jean-Baptiste Lully, 1682)
        *Perseus
    PHA (a); SIM (a)

Persephone (Igor Stravinsky, 1934)
    BAM; BAN; PHA; SIM; TES

Persephone (Antonio Vivaldi, 1955)
    DRE

Perseus SEE Persée

A Persian Market SEE La marché des innocents

Perspective No. 1 SEE Frontier

Peter and the Wolf (Sergei Prokofiev, 1940)
  *Peter und der wolf; *Petîa i Volk; *Piotruś i
  Wilk; *Pyotr i Volk
  BCS (a,i); CRB (a); DRE (i); LAW (a,i,m); PHA; REB (a);
  ROB (a); ROS (i); SEY (x); SIM; TER; TES; TUR (a)

Peter und der Wolf SEE Peter and the Wolf

Petîa i Volk SEE Peter and the Wolf

Les petits riens (Wolfgang Amadeus Mozart, 1778)
  *Drobnostki; *Trifles
  BRI (a); DRE (a); LAW (m); PHA (a); REB (a); REG (a);
  SIM (a); TUR (a)

Petrouchka (Igor Stravinsky, 1911)
  *Petruschka; *Petrushka; *Petrusjka; *Pietruszka
  ASC (a,i); BAI (a); BAL (a,i); BAM(a,i); BAN (a,i);
  BAO (a); BCB (a,i); BRI (i); BRU (i); CLA (i); CRB;
  CRC (a!,i); DAS; DET (i!); DOD (a,i); DRE (i,m); FIS
  (a,i,m!); GOO (a,m); GOU (i!); GRU (a,i); KOC (x); KRO
  (a!,i); LAW (a,i,m!); LAX (a,i); PHA (a,i); REB (a,i);
  REG (a,i); REY (a,i); ROB (a); ROS (i); SEY (x); SIM
  (a,i); STO (i); TER (a); TES (a); TUR (a,i); UNT (i);
  VER; WIN

Petruschka SEE Petrouchka

Petrushka SEE Petrouchka

Petrusjka SEE Petrouchka

Phaedra SEE Phèdre

The Phantom of the Rose SEE Le spectre de la rose

Pharoah's Daughter SEE The Daughter of Pharoah

Phèdre (Georges Auric, 1950)
    *Phaedra
    BAI (a); BBP (a,i); CRB; PHA (i); SIM (l); TES

Physical Things (1966)
    MCD (a)

Piano Concerto No. 2 SEE Ballet Imperial

Piano–Rag–Music (Igor Stravinsky, 1972)
    REZ (b)

Picnic SEE Le déjeuner sur l'herbe

Picnic at Tintagel (Arnold Bax, 1952)
    BAL (a); BAM (a); BAN; CRB; PHA; REZ (a,b,i); SIM; TER;
    TES

Pictures at an Exhibition (Modeste Moussorgsky, 1963)
        *Kartinki s vystavki
    TES

Piece Period (Antonio Vivaldi; Georg Philipp Telemann;
        Franz Joseph Haydn; Ludwig van Beethoven; Antonio
        Francisco Bonporti; Domenico Scarlatti, 1962)
    MCD (a)

The Pied Piper (Aaron Copland, 1951)
    BAL; BAM; BAN; KRO; REZ (a,b,i); TER; TES

Piège de luminère (Jean-Michel Damase, 1952)
        *Light Trap; *Trap of Light
    BAM; BAN; BBT (a,i); CRB; PHA; REZ (a,b,i); SIM; TES

Pierrot lunaire (Arnold Schoenberg, 1962)
        *Ksiezycowy Pierrot
    ASC (a,i); BRI; CLA; MCD (a); TES (i); TUR (a,i)

Pieśń o tesknocie (Adam Swierzyński, 1965)
   TUR (a)

Pieśń o ziemi (Roman Palester, 1937)
   TUR (a)

Pietro Micca (Giovanni Chitti, 1873)
   PHA; SIM

Pietruszka SEE Petrouchka

Pigment (Fritz Geissler, 1960)
   REB (a)

Pillar of Fire (Arnold Schoenberg, 1942)
   BAL (a); BAM (i); BAN; BAO; BBP (a,i); BRI; CRB; CLA
   (i); DAS; KRO (i); LAW (a,i,m); PHA; REY (a,i); ROB
   (a,i); SIM; TER (a); TES (a,i); VER

Pineapple Poll (Arthur Sullivan, 1951)
   BAL; BAM; BAN; BBT (a,i); BRI; CLA (i); CRT (a,i);
   DRE (a); TER; TES

Pinokio (Jadwiga Szajna-Lewandowska, 1964)
   TUR (a)

Piotruś i Wilk SEE Peter and the Wolf

Pity the Poor Dancers SEE The Prospect Before Us

Place (Gordon Mumma, 1966)
   MCD (a)

Les plaisirs de l'hiver (Cesare Pugni, 1849)
      *The Joys of Winter; *Les patineurs
   BCB (a,i); PHA (a); SIM (a)

Plamía líubvi SEE Fiammetta

Plamía parizha SEE The Flames of Paris

Planes (Simone Forti, 1971)
    MCD (a)

Planetomania (Norman Delmuth, 1941)
    DAS

La pléiade perdue SEE Electra

Pli selon pli (Pierre Boulez, 1975)
        *Fold on Fold
    PHA (i); SIM (i)

Plomién Paryzà SEE The Flames of Paris

Pocahontas (Elliott Carter, 1936)
    BCS; REZ (a,b)

Pocalunek wieszczki SEE La baiser de la fée

Podporuchik Kizhe SEE Lieutenant Kije

A Poem Forgotten (Wallingford Riegger, 1970)
    BAN

Poem of Ecstasy SEE Poème de l'extase

Poème de l'extase (Alexander Scriabin, 1970)
        *Poem of Ecstasy
    BAM (a); TES (i)

Poet's Vaudeville (John Herbert McDowell, 1963)
    MCD (a)

Poison Variations (Gwendolyn Watson; Joel Press, 1970)
    MCD (a,i)

Poker Game SEE The Card Party

A Polite Entertainment for Ladies and Gentlemen (Stephen
        Foster, 1975)
    MCD (a)

Polka militaire (Hans Christian Lumbye, 1842)
    ASC (a)

Polovetserdansene fra Fyrst Igor SEE Danses polovtsiennes

Polovtsian dances from 'Prince Igor' SEE Danses
        polovtsiennes

Polowetzer Tänze SEE Danses polovtsiennes

Popoludnie fauna SEE L'après-midi d'un faune

Poppy (1971)
    MCD (a)

Port Said (Konstantine Konstantinov, 1935)
    GOO

The Portents SEE Le prèsages

Portrait of Don Quixote SEE Le portrait de Don Quichotte

Le portrait de Don Quichotte (Goffredo Petrassi, 1947)
      *Portrait of Don Quixote
   PHA; SIM

Portrait of Billie (1960)
   MCD (a)

Porwanie w Tiutiurlistanie (Jadwiga Szajna-Lewandowska, 1967)
   TUR (a)

Pory roku SEE The Seasons (Alexander Glazunov)

Postój kawalerii SEE Cavalry Halt

Potseluǐ fei SEE Le baiser de la fée

Prélude à l'après-midi d'un faune SEE L'après-midi d'un faune

Prelude, Fugue and Riffs (Leonard Bernstein, 1969)
   REZ (b,i)

La premier âge de l'innocence SEE La prima età
      dell'innocenza

Les prèsages (Peter Il'ich Tchaikovsky, 1933)
      *Destiny; *The Portents
   BCB (i); BRU (i); DET (i); DRE; GOO (a,i,m); LAW
   (a,i,m); PHA; SIM; TER; TES; VER

Présence (Bernd Alois Zimmermann, 1968)
   BAM; BRI

The Press (Leopold Wenzel, 1898)
   BCB

Il prigioniero del Caucaso (Caterino Cavos, 1823)
        *Kavkazskiĭ plennik; *L'ombra della fidanzata;
        *The Prisoner in the Caucasus; *The Prisoner of
        the Caucasus; *The Shade of the Betrothed
    PHA (a); SIM (a); VER (a,i)

La prima ballerina (Cesare Pugni, 1849)
        *L'embuscade
    BCB

La prima età dell'innocenza (Louis de Baillou, 1775)
        *The Age of Innocence; *La premier âge de
        l'innocence; *La Rosaia di Salency; *The Rose
        Garden of Salency; *La rosière de Salency
    PHA (a); SIM (a)

Primary Accumulation SEE Accumulation, Primary Accumulation,
    Group Accumulation

Primitive Mysteries (Louis Horst, 1931)
    MCD (a); PHA; SIM

Prince Igor SEE Danses polovtsiennes

The Prince of the Pagodas (Benjamin Britten, 1957)
    CRC (a,i); DRE (a,i,m!); FIS (a,i,m!); PHA; SIM; TER;
    TES

The Princess and the Seven Knights (Anatol Liadov, 1949)
        *Die Prinzessin und die sieben Ritter; *Skazka o
        mertvoĭ tsarevne i semi bogatyriakh
    REB (a)

The Princess and the Swineherd SEE Les cent baisers

Princess Aurora SEE Le mariage d'Aurore

Printemps (Claude Debussy, 1972)
      BAM; REZ (a,b)

Le printemps SEE Vaaren

Prinzessin Turandot (Gottfried von Einem, 1944)
      REB (a); REG (a); WIN

Die Prinzessin und die sieben Ritter SEE The Princess and
      the Seven Knights

The Prisoner in the Caucasus (Boris Asaf'ev) SEE The Prisoner
      of the Caucasus (Boris Asaf'ev)

The Prisoner in the Caucasus (Caterino Cavos) SEE Il
      prigioniero del Caucaso

The Prisoner of the Caucasus (Boris Asaf'ev, 1938)
            *Der Gefangene im Kaukasus; *Kavkazskiĭ plennik;
            *The Prisoner in the Caucasus
      BCS (i); REB (a); STO; TES; VER (a)

The Prisoner of the Caucasus (Caterino Cavos) SEE Il
      prigioniero del Caucaso

The Prisoners (Béla Bartók, 1957)
      BRI; DRE

Prival kavalerii SEE Cavalry Halt

Private Domain (Iannis Xenakis, 1969)
      MCD (a)

The Private Lesson SEE Enetime

The Prodigal Son (Hugo Alfvén) SEE Den förlorade sonen

The Prodigal Son (Sergei Prokofiev) SEE Le fils prodigue

Prologue (William Byrd; Giles Farnaby, and others, 1967)
    BAN; REZ (a,b,i)

Promenade (Franz Joseph Haydn, 1943)
    DAS

Promenade (Maurice Ravel, 1936)
    REZ (a,b)

Prometeo (Ludwig van Beethoven; Wolfgang Amadeus Mozart;
        Franz Joseph Haydn; Joseph Weigl; Salvatore Viganò,
        1813)
    PHA (a,i); SIM (a,i)

Prometeusz SEE Die Geschöpfe des Prometheus

Prometheus SEE Prometeo

Prometheus Bound (Alexander Scriabin, 1929)
    MCD (a)

The Proof of Love SEE L'épreuve d'amour

A Proposal by Advertising SEE Konservatoriet

The Prospect Before Us (William Boyce, 1940)
        *Pity the Poor Dancers
    BAL; BAM; BAN; BCS (a,i); CRB; DAS; DRE (a); LAW; PHA;
    SIM; TER; TES

Protée (Claude Debussy, 1938)
   *Proteus
   DRE; GOO (i,m)

Proteus SEE Protée

Psalmensymfonie (Igor Stravinsky, 1978)
   *Salmesymfonien; *Symphony of Psalms
   ASC (a,i); CLA (i)

Psyché (Jean-Baptiste Lully, 1671)
   PHA (a); SIM (a)

Psyche and Cupid SEE Psyché et l'amour

Psyché et l'amour (1762)
   *Psyche and Cupid
   PHA (a); SIM (a)

Public Garden SEE Jardin public

Pul'chinella SEE Pulcinella

Pulcinella (Igor Stravinsky, after Giovanni Pergolesi, 1920)
   *Pul'chinella; *Punchinello
   BAL; BAM (a); BAN; BAO (a); BCB; BRU (i); DET (i); DRE
   (a); GOO (a,m); KOC (x); LAW (a,m); PHA; REB (a); REG
   (a); REZ (a,b!,i); SIM; STO; TES; TUR (a); WIN

Pulcinella Variations (Igor Stravinsky, 1968)
   BAM; TES

Punch and the Child (Richard Arnell, 1947)
   REZ (a,b,i)

Punchinello SEE Pulcinella

Die Puppenfee (Josef Bayer, 1888)
     *The Fairy Doll
     PHA (a); REB (a); REG (a); SIM (a); WIN

Push Comes to Shove (Joseph Lamb; Franz Joseph Haydn, 1976)
     ASC (a,i); BAM (a); CLA (i); PHA; REY (a,i); SIM

Pygmalion (Jean-Philippe Rameau, 1748)
     PHA (a); SIM (a)

Pytor i volk SEE Peter and the Wolf

Qarrtsiluni (Knudåge Riisager, 1942)
     ASC (a,i); BBP (a,i)

Quartet (Sergei Prokofiev, 1954)
     REZ (a,b)

Les quatre saisons (Cesare Pugni, 1848)
     BCB (a,i)

Quatuor (Dmitri Shostakovich, 1964)
     REZ (a,b)

The Queen of Spades (Peter Il'ich Tchaikovsky, 1978)
     PHA; SIM

Quelques fleurs (Daniel Auber, 1948)
     DRE; LAW (a,i,m)

The Quest (William Walton, 1943)
     CRB; DAS

Quilt, Revised (1971)
     MCD (a)

Quintet (Laura Nyro, 1968)
    MCD (a)

Radha (Léo Delibes, 1906)
    MCD (a); SHE (a,i)

Raggedy Ann and Raggedy Andy (John Alden Carpenter, 1974)
    TES

Ragtime (I) (Igor Stravinsky, 1960)
    BAN; REZ (b,i)

Ragtime (II) (Igor Stravinsky, 1967)
    REZ (a,b,i)

Raïmonda SEE Raymonda

Rainbow 'Round My Shoulder (1959)
    MCD (a)

Rainforest (David Tudor, 1968)
    MCD (a)

Rajmonda SEE Raymonda

The Rake's Progress (Gavin Gordon, 1935)
        *Das Leben eines Wüstlings
    BAL; BAM; BAN; BCB (i); BRI (i); CLA (i); CRB (i); DAS;
    DRE; PHA (i); REB (a); REG (a,i); SIM (i); TER; TES; VER

Random Breakfast (1963)
    MCD

Raoul de Créquis (Caterino Cavos; Sushkov, 1819)
        *Raul' de Kreki; *The Return from the Crusades
    BCS

Raul' de Kreki SEE Raoul de Créquis

Rapsodie espagnole (Maurice Ravel, 1975)
    REA (a,b!,i)

Raymonda (Alexander Glazunov, 1898)
        *Raĭmonda; *Rajmonda
    ASC (a); BAM (a); BAM; BCB; BRI; CLA (i); CRB; KER: LAW
    (i,m); PHA; REB (a); REG (a); SIM: STO (i); TER; TES
    (i); TUR (a)

Raymonda Variations (Alexander Glazunov, 1961)
        *Valses et variations
    BAM; BAN; REZ (a,b!,i); TES

Re-moves (1966)
    MCD (a)

The Real McCoy (George Gershwin, 1974)
    BAM

Das Recht des Herrn (Victor Bruns, 1953)
        *Jus primae noctis
    REB (a)

Recital for Cellist and Eight Dancers SEE Recital for Cello
        and Eight Dancers

Recital for Cello and Eight Dancers (Johann Sebastian Bach,
        1964)
            *Recital for Cellist and Eight Dancers
    TES

Red and Black SEE Le rouge et noir

The Red Detachment of Women (1964)
    TES

The Red Flower SEE The Red Poppy

Red Lights, Green Lights, SEE Feux rouges, feux verts

The Red Poppy (Reinhold Glière, 1927)
        *Czerwony mak; *Krasnyĭ mak; *The Red Flower;
        *Roter Mohn
    BCB (i); CRB; LAW (i,m); PHA (i); REB (a); SIM (i);
    STO; TES; TUR (a)

Red Sails SEE Crimson Sails

Reflections (Peter Il'ich Tchaikovsky, 1971)
    BAM

Reflections in the Park (Gary McFarland, 1964)
    MCD (a)

The Rehearsal (Morton Gould, 1965)
    TES

Relâche (Erik Satie, 1924)
    BCB (a,i); PHA (i); SIM (i)

The Relativity of Icarus (Gerhard Samuel, 1974)
    BAM (a); TES

Remembrances (Richard Wagner, 1973)
    BAM (a); BAO (a); TES

Reminiscence (Benjamin Godard, 1935)
    REZ (a,b)

Le renard (Igor Stravinsky, 1922)
        *Baĭka; *The Fox; *Lis

BAI (a); DRE (a); KOC (x); PHA; REZ (a,b,i); SIM;
TUR (a,i)

La rencontre (Henri Sauguet, 1948)
        *Edipe et la Sphinx
    BBP (a,i)

Le rendez-vous (Joseph Kosma, 1945)
    BBT (a)

Les rendez-vous (Daniel Auber, 1933)
        *Les rendezvous
    BAL; BAM; BAN; CLA (i); DRE; PHA; SIM; TER; TES

Le rendez-vous manque (Michel Magne, 1958)
        *The Broken Date
    TER

Les rendezvous SEE Les rendez-vous

Requiem SEE Maledictions et lumiéres

Requiem Canticles (I) (Igor Stravinsky, 1968)
    REZ (a,b,i)

Requiem Canticles (II) (Igor Stravinsky, 1972)
    BAM (a); BAO (a); REZ (a,b,i)

Le retour (Sergei Prokofiev, 1954)
    DRE

The Return from the Crusades SEE Raoul de Créquis

The Return of Springtime (Cesare Bossi, 1965)
    BRI (a,i)

Revanche (Giuseppe Verdi, 1951)
        *Revenge; *Vendetta
    BAL; BAM; BAN; BBP (i); PHA; SIM; TER; TES

Revelations (1960)
        *Abenbaringer
    ASC (a,i); GRU (a,i); MCD (a); REY (a,i)

Revenge SEE Revanche

Reveries (Peter Il'ich Tchaikovsky, 1969)
        *Tchaikovsky Suite No. 1; *Tschaikovsky Suite No. 1
    BAM (a); BAO (a); REZ (a,b,i); TES

The Revolt in the Harem SEE La révolte au sérail

The Revolt in the Seraglio SEE La révolte au sérail

La révolte au sérail (Théodore Labarre, 1833)
        *The Revolt in the Harem; *The Revolt in the
        Seraglio
    BCB (a); PHA (a); SIM (a)

Rhapsody (Sergei Rachmaninov, 1980)
    CLA (i)

Rhapsody in Blue (George Gershwin, 1928)
    BCB (a); GOO (a,m)

The Rib of Eve (Morton Gould, 1956)
    TER

Ricercare (Mordecai Seter, 1966)
    TES

Rigonda (Romaul'd Grinblat, 1959)
   STO (i)

Rinaldo and Armida (Malcolm Arnold, 1955)
   BBP (a,i); CRB (i); DRE; TER; TES

The Rite of Spring SEE Le sacre du printemps

Rites de passage (Paquita Anderson, 1941)
   MCD (a)

Il ritorno di Agamennone (1789)
         *Agamemnon's Return
   PHA (a); SIM (a)

Rituals (Béla Bartók, 1975)
   BAM

The River (Duke Ellington, 1970)
   BAM (a); BAO (a); PHA; SIM; TES

Road of the Phoebe Snow (Duke Ellington; Billy Strayhorn,
         1959)
   MCD (a); TES

Roads to Hell (Geneviève Pitot, 1941)
   MCD (a)

Robert Schumann's Davidsbündlertänze SEE Davidsbündlertänze

Rocks (1967)
   MCD (a)

Rodeo (Aaron Copland, 1942)
         *The Courting at Burnt Ranch; *Das Liebeswerben
         auf der Burnt Ranch

BAL (a,i); BAM (a); BAN (i); BAO (a); BBT (a,i); CLA;
CRB; DRE; GRU (a,i); KRO (i); LAW (i,m); REB (a); ROB
(a); SEY (x); TER (i); TES; TUR (a); UNT (i); VER (a,i)

Rodin brought to life SEE Rodin mis en vie

Rodin mis en vie (Michael Kamen, 1974)
        *Rodin brought to life
        BAM; PHA; SIM

Le roi candaule (Cesare Pugni, 1868)
        BCB

Le roi nu (Jean Françaix, 1936)
        *Des Kaisers neue Kleider; *Des Königs neue
        Kleider; *Der nackte König
        BCS (a,i); REB (a); REG (a); WIN

Roma (Georges Bizet, 1955)
        REZ (a,b,i); TER

Romance (Johannes Brahms, 1971)
        BAM; TES

Romantic Age (Vincenzo Bellini, 1942)
        LAW

Romeo and Juliet (Hector Berlioz, 1966)
        PHA; SIM

Romeo and Juliet (Frederick Delius, 1943)
        BAL (a); BAM (a); BAN; BBP (a,i); DAS; DRE; KRO (i);
        LAW (a,i,m); ROB (a,i)

Romeo and Juliet (Constant Lambert, 1926)
        DET (i); KOC (x); PHA; SIM

Romeo and Juliet (Sergei Prokofiev, 1938)
        *Roméo et Juliette; *Romeo i Dsjuljetta; *Romeo i
        Dzhul'etta; *Romeo i Julia; *Romeo og Julie;
        *Romeo und Julia
        ASC (a!,i); BAM (a,i,b); BAN (a,i); BAO (a!); BCS (i);
        BOL (i!); BRI (a,i); CLA (a!,i!); DAC (a,i!); DOD (a,i);
        DRE (a); GRU (a,i); KER (a,i); LAW (m); LAX (a,i); PHA
        (a,i); REB (a,i); REG (a); REY (a,i); SIM (a,i); STO
        (i); TER (a,i); TES (a,i); TUR (a,i); VER (a); WIN

Romeo and Juliet (Peter Il'ich Tchaikovsky, 1938)
        BCS

Roméo e Juliette SEE Romeo and Juliet (Sergei Prokofiev)

Romeo i Dsjuljetta SEE Romeo and Juliet (Sergei Prokofiev)

Romeo i Dzhul'etta SEE Romeo and Juliet (Sergei Prokofiev)

Romeo i Julia SEE Romeo and Juliet (Sergei Prokofiev)

Romeo og Julie SEE Romeo and Juliet (Sergei Prokofiev)

Romeo und Julia SEE Romeo and Juliet (Sergei Prokofiev)

Rondo vom goldenen Kalb (Gottfried von Einem, 1952)
        REG (a)

Roof Piece (1971)
        MCD (a)

Rooms (Kenyon Hopkins, 1955)
        BAM; MCD; REY (a,i)

Ropes (Charles Ives, 1961)
        TES

The Ropes of Time (Jan Boerman, 1970)
    BAM; PHA; SIM

La rosaia di Salency SEE La prima età dell'innocenza

La rose des vents (Darius Milhaud, 1958)
    TER

A Rose for Miss Emily (Alan Hovhaness, 1970)
    BAM; TES

The Rose Garden of Salency SEE La prima età dell'innocenza

Rose Latulippe (Harry Freedman, 1966)
    TES (i)

La rose malade (Gustav Mahler, 1973)
    *O Rose, Thou Art Sick
    BAM; PHA (i); SIM (i); TES

The Rose of Lahore SEE Lalla rookh

Rosendrømmen SEE Le spectre de la rose

Rosenkranz (Ahti Sonninen, 1959)
    REB (a,i)

Rosida (Cesare Pugni, 1845)
      *Les mines de Syracuse
    BCB (a)

La Rosière de Salency SEE La prima età dell'innocenza

Le rossignol SEE Le chant du rossignol

Le rossignol et la rose (Jānis Kalniņš, 1938)
      *The Nightingale and the Rose
   BCS (i)

Der rote Mantel (Luigi Nono, 1954)
   WIN

Roter Mohn SEE The Red Poppy

Le rouge et noir (Dmitri Shostakovich, 1939)
      *L'étrange farandole; *Red and Black; *The Strange
      Farandole
   BCS; DET (i); GOO (i,m); LAW (a,i,m);ROB; SEY (x); TER;
   TES

La Roussalka (Lucien Lambert, 1911)
   BET

Route 6 (1972)
   MCD (a)

Ruses d'amour (Alexander Glazunov, 1900)
      *Baryshnia-sluzhanka; *Ispytanie damisa; *Love's
      Trickery
   BCB; LAW (a,m); PHA; SIM; STO

Les ruses de l'amour SEE La toilette de Vénus

Russian Dolls SEE Igrouchka

Russian Heroes SEE Bogatyri

Russian Soldier (Sergei Prokofiev, 1942)
   LAW (a,i,m); SEY (x)

Russian Toys SEE Igrouchka

Rybak i jego narzeczona SEE Napoli

Sacountala (Ernest Reyer, 1858)
    BCB (a,i); PHA; SIM

Le sacre de printemps SEE Le sacre du printemps

Le sacre du printemps (Igor Stravinsky, 1913)
        *Forårets helliggorelse; *Das Frülingsopfer; *Der
        Frühlingsweihe; *The rite of Spring; *Le sacre de
        printemps; *Swieto wiosny; *Vesna svîashchennaîa
    ASC (a,i); BAI (a); BAL; BAM (a,i); BAN; BAO (a); BCB;
    BRI; CLA (a,i); CRB; DAS; DRE (a,m); GOO (a,m);
    GRU (a,i); KOC (x); LAW (a,m); PHA (a,i); REB (a,i);
    REG (a,i); REY (a,i); ROB (a,i); SIM (a,i); STO; TER;
    TES; TUR (a,i); UNT (i); WIN

Sacred Grove on Mount Tamalpais (Alan Raph; Johann
        Pachelbel, 1972)
    BAM (a,i); BAO (a); TES

Sadako (Jean Kurt Forest, 1964)
    REB (a)

The Sailors SEE Les matelots

The Sailor's Return (Arthur Oldham, 1947)
    BBT (a,i); CRB

Saint Francis SEE Nobilissima visione

Saint George and the Dragon (1976)
    PHA (i); SIM (i)

Les saisons SEE The Seasons (Alexander Glazunov)

Sakta der Freiheit (Adolf Skulté, 1950)
    *Sakta svobody
    REB (a); STO

Sakta svobody SEE Sakta der Freiheit

Salade (Darius Milhaud, 1924)
    BAI (a); CRB; PHA; SIM; TES

Salammbô (Andrei Arends, 1910)
    PHA; SIM

Salmesymfonien SEE Psalmensymfonie

Salome (Lester Horton, 1938)
    *The Face of Violence
    MCD (a)

Salomé (Florent Schmitt, 1907)
    KOC (x)

El salón México (Aaron Copland, 1943)
    LAW (m)

Saltarelli (Antonio Vivaldi, 1974)
    BAM; REZ (a,b); TES

Sampo (Gel'mer Sinisalo, 1959)
    STO

Sanctum (Alwin Nikolais, 1964)
    MCD (a,i)

Les santons (Henri Tomasi, 1938)
    BAI (a)

Sarabande (François Couperin, 1965)
    BAN

Sarabande and Danse (I) (Claude Debussy, 1970)
    REZ (a,b,i)

Sarabande and Danse (II) (Claude Debussy, 1975)
    BAM; REZ (b)

Saratoga (Jaromir Weinberger, 1941)
    SEY (x)

Sargasso (Ernst Křenek, 1964)
    TES

Satisfyin' Lover (1967)
    MCD (a)

Saudades (Denis ApIvor, 1955)
    DRE

Scaramouche (Jean Sibelius, 1922)
        *Skaramuš
    BCS (i); REB (a)

Scènes de ballet (Igor Stravinsky, 1944)
        *Scènes du ballet
    BAL; BAM; BAN; BRI; CLA; DRE; LAW; REG (a); REZ
    (a,b,i); TER; TES

Scènes du ballet SEE Scènes de ballet

Scenes of Childhood SEE Kinderszenen

Schachmatt SEE Checkmate

Schéhérazade SEE Shéhérazade (Nikolai Rimsky-Korsakov)

Scherzo à la russe (Igor Stravinsky, 1972)
    REZ (a,b,i); TES

Scherzo fantastique (Igor Stravinsky, 1972)
    BAM; REZ (a,b,i); TES

Scherzo for Massah Jack (Charles Ives, 1973)
    BAM

Scherzo Waltz SEE Hoop Dance

Schlagobers (Richard Strauss, 1924)
    BCB; REB (a); REG (a); WIN

Schneewittchen (Karl-Rudi Griesbach, 1956)
    REB (a)

The School of Ballet SEE Scuola di ballo

Die Schöpfung der Welt SEE La création du monde

Schubert Variations (Franz Schubert, 1972)
    TES

Schubertiade (Franz Schubert, 1970)
    BAM (a); TES

Schumann Concerto (Robert Schumann, 1951)
    BAL; BAM; BAN; DRE

Schuraleh (Farid ÎArullin, 1945)
        *Shurale; *Shuraleh
    REB (a); STO (i); TES

Schwanensee SEE Swan Lake

Der Schweizer Milchmädchen (Adalbert Gyrowetz; Michele
        Caraffa, 1821)
        *La laitière suisse; *Nathalie; *The Swiss Milkmaid
    BCB

Scotch Symphony (Felix Mendelssohn, 1952)
    BAL; BAM (a); BAN (i); DRE (a); KOR; REZ (a,b!i); TER;
    TES

Scudorama (Charles Jackson, 1963)
    MCD (a)

Scuola di ballo (Luigi Boccherini, 1924)
        *École de danse; *The School of Ballet
    BCB; BRU (i); DET (i); GOO (i,m)

Sea Change (Benjamin Britten, 1972)
    BAM

Sea Change (Jean Sibelius, 1949)
    CRB; DRE

Sea Shadow (Michael Colgrass or Maurice Ravel, 1962)
    BAM; BAN (i); TES

The Seasons (John Cage, 1947)
    REZ (a,b)

The Seasons (Alexander Glazunov, 1900)
        *Die Jahreszeiten; *Pory roku; *Les saisons;
        *Vremena goda
    BAM; BAO; BCB; DRE (a); LAW (m); PHA; REB (a); SIM;
    STO; TES; TUR (a)

Sebastian (Gian-Carlo Menotti, 1944)
BAM; BAN; ROB (a); TER; TES (i)

Second Piano Concerto in G Major SEE Ballet Imperial

Secret Places (Wolfgang Amadeus Mozart, 1968)
BAM; TES

Sed'maĩa simfoniĩa SEE Leningrad Symphony

Selina (Gioacchino Rossini, 1948)
CRB; DRE

Sem' krasaviṱs SEE The Seven Beauties

Semiramide (Christoph Willibald von Gluck, 1765)
*Semiramis
PHA (a); SIM (a)

Semiramis SEE Semiramide

Sen SEE The Dream

Sephardic Song SEE Sephardic Songs

Sephardic Songs (1974)
*Sephardic Song
BAM; TES

Septet Extra (Camille Saint-Saëns, 1973)
ASC (a,i)

La septième symphonie (Ludwig van Beethoven, 1938)
*The Seventh Symphony

BCS (a,i); DET (i); DRE; GOO (a,i!,m); LAW (a,i,m);
PHA; ROB (a); SEY (x); SIM; TER; TES

Les septs péchés capitaux (Kurt Weill, 1933)
*The Seven Deadly Sins; *Die sieben Todsünden der
Kleinbürger; *De syv Dødssynder
ASC (a); BAM; BAN; BBP (a,i); PHA; REB (a); REZ
(a,b!,i); SIM; TER (a,i); TES; WIN

Septuor (Jean Lutèce, 1950)
BBP (i)

Serait—ce la mort? (Richard Strauss, 1970)
*Could This Be Death?
PHA; SIM

Seraphic Dialogue (Norman Dello Joio, 1955)
MCD (a); REY (a,i)

Serce z piernika SEE Licitarsko srce

Serdtse gor SEE The Heart of the Hills

Serenade (Peter Il'ich Tchaikovsky, 1934)
ASC (a,i); BAL (a); BAM (a); BAN (a); BAO (a); BRI (i);
CLA (i); DOD (a,i); DRE (i); GRU (a,i); KRO; LAW (i,m);
PHA; REY (a,i); REZ (a,b!,i); SEY (x); SIM; TER;
TES (i)

Serenade in A (Igor Stravinsky, 1972)
BAM; REZ (a,b,i)

Serpent Heart SEE Cave of the Heart

Serpentine (Ernest? Gillet, 1891)
MCD (a)

Session '58 SEE Session for Six

Session for Six (Teo Macero, 1958)
        *Session '58
    MCD (a)

The Seven Beauties (Kara Karaev, 1952)
        *Sem' krasavi͡ts; *Die sieben Schönen
    REB (a); STO

The Seven Deadly Sins SEE Les septs péchés capitaux

The Seventh Symphony SEE La sèptieme symphonie

The Shade SEE L'ombre

The Shade of the Betrothed SEE Il prigioniero del Caucaso

The Shadow (Ernö Dohnányi, 1952)
    BBT (a,i); DRE (a)

Shadow of the Wind (Gustav Mahler, 1948)
    BAM; BAN; DRE; LAW (a,i,m)

Shadow'd Ground (Aaron Copland, 1965)
    BAN; REZ (a,b,i)

Shadowplay (Charles Koechlin, 1967)
    BAM; BAN; BRI (i); TES

The Shakers (1930)
        *Dance of the Chosen
    MCD (a); REY (a,i); TES

Shakespeare (Paolo Giorza, 1955)
    *A Midsummer Night's Dream; *Il sogno di una notte
    d'estate
  PHA; SIM

Shakuntala (Sergei Balasanian, 1963)
    STO (i)

Shar ptiza SEE L'oiseau de feu

Shchelkunchik SEE The Nutcracker

Shéhérazade (Nikolai Rimsky-Korsakov, 1910)
    *Schéhérazade; *Shekherazada; *Szecherezada
  ASC (a); BAI (a); BAL (a,i); BAM (a,i); BAN (a,i); BCB
  (a,i); BRI; BRU (i); CLA; CRB; DAS; DET (i!); DRE (a);
  GOO (a,i,m); KOC (x); KRO (i); LAW (a,i,m); PHA (a,i);
  REB (a); REG (a); ROB (a); SEY (x); SIM (a,i); STO;
  TER; TES; TUR (a,i); UNT (i); WIN

Shéhérazade (Maurice Ravel, 1975)
    BAM; REZ (b)

Shekherazada SEE Shéhérazade (Nikolai Rimsky-Korsakov)

The Shining People of Leonard Cohen (Harry Freedman, 1971)
    TES

Shirah (Alan Hovhaness, 1960)
    MCD (a)

Shopeniana SEE Les sylphides

Shore of Happiness SEE Coast of Happiness

The Shore of Hope SEE Coast of Hope

Shostakovich Seventh Symphony SEE Leningrad Symphony

Show Piece (Robert McBride, 1937)
    REZ (a,b,i)

Shrove Tuesday SEE Mardi Gras

Shurale SEE Schuraleh

Shuraleh SEE Schuraleh

Shut SEE The Buffoon

Sieba (Romualdo Marenco, 1876)
        *La spada di Wodan; *The Sword of Wotan
    BCB; PHA (a); SIM (a)

Die sieben Schönen SEE The Seven Beauties

Die sieben Todsünden der Kleinbürger SEE Les septs péchés
        capitaux

Signals II (1971)
    MCD

Simple Symphony (Benjamin Britten, 1944)
    DRE (i)

Sinfonietta (Paul Hindemith, 1975)
    REZ (b)

Sinfonietta (Malcolm Williamson, 1967)
    BAM; BAN

Les sirenes (Lord Berners, 1946)
    CRB (a); DAS

Sisyfos (Karl-Birger Blomdahl, 1957)
        *Sisyphus
    TES

Sisyphus SEE Sisyfos

16 Millimeter Earrings (1966)
    MCD (a)

Sjtjelkuntjik SEE The Nutcracker

En Skaersommernatdsdrøm SEE Ein Sommernachtstraum

Skaramuss SEE Scaramouche

The Skaters SEE Les patineurs

Skating Rink (Arthur Honegger, 1922)
    BCB (i)

Skazka o beglom soldate i cherte SEE L'histoire du soldat

Skazka o mertvoĭ t͡sarevne i semi bogatyrĭakh SEE The
        Princess and the Seven Knights

Skazka o pope i rabotnike ego Balde SEE The Tale of the
        Priest and His Workman Balde

Skazka pro shuta SEE The Buffoon

Sklakiem gromu SEE The Path of Thunder

Sklaven (Wolfgang Hohensee, 1962)
       *Das Fanal
       REB (a!,i)

Skyscrapers (John Alden Carpenter, 1926)
       BCB (i); LAW (m)

Slaughter on Tenth Avenue (Richard Rodgers, 1936)
       BAL; BAN; REZ (a,b,i); TES

The Sleeping Beauty (Henri Dutilleux) SEE La belle au bois
       dormant (Henri Dutilleux)

The Sleeping Beauty (Louis Hérold) SEE La belle au bois
       dormant (Louis Hérold)

The Sleeping Beauty (Peter Il'ich Tchaikovsky, 1890)
       *La belle au bois dormant; *Bluebird pas de deux;
       *Dornröschen; *Grand pas d'action; *The Sleeping
       Princess; *Spiaca królewna; *Spiaschaia krasavitsa;
       *Spjasjtjaja krasavitsa; *Tornerose
       ASC (a!,i); BAI (a); BAL (a!,i); BAM (a!b,i); BAN (a); BAO
       (a!); BCB (a!,i); BOL (a,i!); BRI (a!,i); CLA (a!,i); CRB
       (a); CRT (a,i!); DAC (a,i!); DAS (a); DOD (i); DRE
       (a,m); EWE (a); FIS (a!,m!); GOU (i!); GRU (a,i); KER
       (i); KOC (x); KRO (a!,i); LAW (a,i,m!); LAX (a,i); PHA
       (a,i); REB (a,i); REG (a,i); REY (a,i); ROB (a!,i); ROS
       (i); SIM (a,i); STO (i); TER; TES (a,i); TUR (a,i); UNT
       (i); VER (a); WIN

The Sleeping Princess SEE The Sleeping Beauty (Peter Il'ich
       Tchaikovsky)

The Sleepwalker SEE La somnambule (Louis Hérold)

Den slet bevogtede datter SEE La fille mal gardée

The Smugglers SEE Stella

Soaring (Robert Schumann, 1920)
    MCD (a)

The Soft-boiled Egg SEE L'oeuf à la coque

Un sogno SEE Beatrice di Gand

Il sogno di una notte d'estate SEE Shakespeare

Un soir (Florent Schmitt, 1937)
    DET (i)

Soir de fête (Léo Delibes, 1925)
         *Soirée de fête
    DET (x)

Soirée de fête SEE Soir de fête

Soirée musicale (Gioacchino Rossini, 1938)
         *Soirées musicales
    DRE (a)

Soirées musicales SEE Soirée musicale

The Soldier and the Gypsy (Manuel de Falla, 1936)
    REZ (b)

Soldiers' Mass (Bohuslav Martinů, 1980)
         *Field Mass
    CLA (i)

The Soldier's Story SEE L'historie du soldat

The Soldier's Tale SEE L'historie du soldat

Le soleil de minuit SEE Le soleil de nuit

Le soleil de nuit (Nikolai Rimsky-Korsakov, 1915)
        *The Midnight Sun; *Le soleil de minuit
    DET (x); GOO (a,i,m); KOC (x); PHA; SIM

Solitaire (Malcolm Arnold, 1956)
    ASC (i); BAM; BAN; DRE (a,i); TER; TES

Solo for Voice I (John Cage, 1968)
    BRI

Soloveĭ SEE The Nightingale (Mikhail Kroshner)

Solusjka SEE Cinderella (Sergei Prokofiev)

Solveig SEE The Ice Maiden

Solyushka SEE Cinderella (Boris Shel)

El sombrero de tres picos SEE The Three-cornered Hat

Sombreros (Ivan Boutnikoff, 1956)
    TER

Some Times (Claus Ogerman, 1972)
    BAM; TES

Ein sommernachtstraum (Felix Mendelssohn, 1977)
        *En Skaersommernatsdrøm
    ASC (a,i)

Ein Sommertag (Werner Egk, 1950)
    REG (a)

La somnambule (Louis Hérold, 1827)
        *L'arrivée d'un nouveau seigneur; *A New Lord
        Comes; *The Sleepwalker
    BCB (a,i); PHA (a); SIM (a)

La somnambule (Vittorio Rieti) SEE Night Shadow

Somnambulism (Stan Kenton; Pete Rugolo, 1953)
        *Abstraction; *Lament; *Monotony
    DRE (a)

Sonata for Eight Easy Pieces (Igor Stravinsky, 1974)
    TES

Sonate à trois (Béla Bartók, 1957)
    BRI

Sonatine (Maurice Ravel, 1975)
    BAM; REZ (a,b!,i)

Song of a Wayfarer SEE Chant du compagnon errant

The Song of the Earth SEE Das Lied von der Erde

Song of the Heiducks (Alexander Raitschev, 1953)
        *Heiduckenlied
    REB (a)

The Song of the Nightingale SEE Le chant du rossignol

Song of the Wayfarer SEE Chant du compagnon errant

Songes (Darius Milhaud, 1933)
        *Dreams
    REZ (a,b)

Songs for Young Lovers (1965)
    MCD

Songs, Lamentations and Praises (Geoffry Burgon, 1979)
    PHA; SIM

Songs of a Wayfarer SEE Chant du compagnon errant

La sonnambula SEE Night Shadow

La source (Léo Delibes; Léon Minkus, 1866)
        *The Spring
    BAM (a); BCB (a); DRE (a); PHA; REZ (a,b,i); SIM

Souvenirs (Samuel Barber, 1955)
    BAM; BAN; KRO; REZ (a,b,i); TER; TES (i)

Søvngaengersken SEE Night Shadow

Soweto (1977)
    PHA (i); SIM (i)

La spada di Wodan SEE Sieba

Spanish Caprice SEE Capriccio espagnol

Spartacus (Aram Khachaturian, 1956)
        *Spartak; * Spartakus
    BAM (a,i); BAO (a); BOL (a,i!); CLA (a,i); DOD (a,i);
    GRU (a,i); PHA (i); REB (a); SIM (i); STO (i); TES;
    TUR (a,i)

Spartak SEE Spartacus

Spartakus SEE Spartacus

Le spectre de la rose (Carl Maria von Weber, 1911)
*Duch rózy; *Der Geist der Rose; *The Phantom of
the Rose; *Rosendrømmen; *The Spirit of the Rose
ASC (a); BAI (a); BAL (a); BAM (a,i); BAN; BAO; BCB
(a,i); BRI; BRU (i); CLA (i); CRB; CRC (a,i); DAS; DET
(i); DRE (a); GOO (a,i,m); GRU (a,i); KOC (x); LAW (i,m);
PHA; REB (a); REG (a); REY (a,i); ROB; ROS (i); SEY (x);
SIM; TER; TES (i); TUR (a); UNT (i); VER; WIN

The Spellbound Child SEE L'enfant et les sortilèges

Spiaca Królewna SEE The Sleeping Beauty (Peter Il'ich
Tchaikovsky)

Spiashchaia krasavitsa SEE The Sleeping Beauty (Peter Il'ich
Tchaikovsky)

The Spider's Banquet SEE Le festin de l'araignée

Spiele SEE Jeux

The Spirit of the Rose SEE Le spectre de la rose

The Spirit of the Sea (Roy S. Stoughton, 1923)
SHE (a,i)

The Spirit Seeker SEE La chercheuse d'esprit

The Spirits of the Mountain SEE Ballet des montagnards

Spjasjtjaja krasavitsa SEE The Sleeping Beauty (Peter Il'ich
Tchaikovsky)

Spookride, Version II (Frédéric Chopin; Ezra Sims; and
others, 1970)
MCD (a)

Sport (Romualdo Marenco, 1897)
    PHA; SIM

The Spring SEE La source

Spring Song (Felix Mendelssohn, 1903)
    MCD (a)

A Spring Tale (Fritz Cohen, 1939)
    BCS (a,i)

Spring Waters (Sergei Rachmaninov)
    REY (a,i)

Der Springbrunnen von Bachtschissarai SEE The Fountain of
        Bakhchisarai

Square Dance (Steve Reich, 1973)
    MCD (a)

Square Dance (Arcangelo Corelli; Antonio Vivaldi, 1957)
    BAM (a); BAN; REZ (a,b!,i); TER (i); TES

Squares (Erik Satie, 1969)
    BAM

St. Francis SEE Nobilissima visione

Stabat mater (Kryzsztof Penderecki, 1976)
    PHA; SIM

A Stableboy's Dream SEE The Filly

Stages (Arne Nordheim; Bob Downes, 1971)
    PHA; SIM

Der stählerne Schritt SEE Pas d'acier

Stal'noĭ skok SEE Pas d'acier

Stalowy krok SEE Pas d'acier

The Stars (Anton Simon, 1898)
    *Zvezdy
   BBP

Stars and Stripes (John Philip Sousa, 1958)
    BAM; BAN (a); BRI; CLA (i); GRU (a,i); REY (a,i); REZ
    (a,b!i); TER (a,i); TES

The Steadfast Tin Soldier (Georges Bizet, 1975)
    BAM; REZ (a,b,i)

The Steel Trot SEE Pas d'acier

Die steinerne Blume SEE The Stone Flower

Der steinerne Gast SEE Don Juan (Christoph Willibald von
    Gluck, 1761)

Stella (Cesare Pugni, 1850)
    *Les contrebandiers; *The Smugglers
   BCB (i)

Stenka Razine (Alexander Glazunov, 1943)
    DET (i); PHA; SIM

The Still Point (Claude Debussy, 1954)
    BAM (a); BAO (a); PHA; REY (a,i); REZ (a,b,i); SIM;
    TER; TES

Stimmung (Karlheinz Stockhausen, 1972)
      BAM

The Stone Flower (Sergei Prokofiev, 1954)
         *Kamennyĭ ĉsvetok; *Kamienny kwait; *Die stienerne
         Blume
      BAM (a); BAN; BOL (i!); CLA; PHA; REB (a); SIM; STO
      (i); TER; TES; TUR (a,i)

Das Störchlein SEE The Little Stork

La strada (Rinaldi Rota, 1966)
         *The Street
      PHA; SIM

Der Stralauer Fischzug (Leo Spies, 1936)
      REB (a)

The Strange Farandole SEE Le rouge et noir

The Strange Festival SEE La fête étrange

Strange Hero (Stan Kenton; Pete Rugolo, 1948)
      MCD

Stravinsky: Symphony in C (Igor Stravinsky, 1967)
         *Symphony in C
      REZ (a,b,i)

Stravinsky Violin Concerto SEE Violin Concerto

The Street SEE La strada

Street Games (Jacques Ibert, 1952)
      BBT (i); BRI; TES; VER

A **Streetcar Named Desire** (Alex North, 1952)
   BAL; BAN; KRO; TER (i); TES (i)

The Streletsy Revolt SEE Gli Strelizzi

Gli Strelizzi (1809)
       *The Streletsy Revolt
   BCB (i); PHA (a); SIM (a)

Strolling Players SEE Les forains

Stworzenie świata SEE La création du monde

Suite de danses (Frédéric Chopin)
   DET (x)

Suite en blanc (Édouard Lalo, 1943)
       *Noir et blanc
   BAI (a); BRI; CLA; PHA (i); SIM (i); TES

Suite for Five SEE Suite for Five in Space and Time

Suite for Five in Space and Time (John Cage, 1956)
       *Suite for Five
   MCD (a)

Suite No. 3 (Peter Il'ich Tchaikovsky, 1970)
       *Tchaikovsky Suite No. 3
   BAM (i); CLA; REZ (a,b!,i); TES

Summer Interlude (Ottorino Respighi, 1950)
   CRB; DRE

Summerspace (Morton Feldman, 1958)
   BAM; BAN; GRU (a,i); PHA; REY (a,i); REZ (a,b,i); SIM;
   TES

Sun into Darkness (Malcolm Williamson, 1966)
   BRI

Superantics '70 (Alwin Nikolais, 1970)
   MCD (a)

Suspension (Ray Green, 1943)
   MCD (a)

Svadebka SEE Les noces

Svanesøen SEE Swan Lake

Svetlana (Dmitri Klebanov, 1939)
   BCS (i)

Svetlyĭ rucheĭ SEE The Bright Stream

Swan Lake (Peter Il'ich Tchaikovsky, 1877)
        *Jezioro labedzie; *Le lac de cygnes; *Lebedinoe
        ozero; *Lebedinoje osero; *Schwanensee; *Svanesøen
        ASC (a!,i); BAI (a); BAL (a!,i); BAM (a!,b,i); BAN
        (a,i); BAO (a,!); BCB (a,i); BOL (a,i!); BRI (a!,i);
        BRU; CLA (a!,i!); CRB (a,i); CRT (a,i!); DAC (a,i!);
        DAS (a); DET (i); DOD (a,i); DRE (a,i,m); EWE (a); FIS
        (a,i,m!); GOO (a,i,m); GOU (i!); GRU (a,i); KER (a,i);
        KOC (x); KRO (a,i); LAW (a,i,m!); LAX (a,i); PHA (a,i);
        REB (a!); REG (a,i); REZ (a,b!,i); REY (a,i); ROB (a!);
        ROS (i); SEY (x); SIM (a,i); STO (i); TER (a,i); TES
        (a,i); TUR (a,i); UNT (i); VER (a,i); VIV (a,i); WIN

Świeto ognia (Zygmunt Noskowski, 1902)
   TUR (a)

Świeto wiosny SEE Le sacre du printemps

The Swiss Milkmaid SEE Der Schweizer Milchmädchen

Świtezianka (Eugeniusz Morawski–Dabrowa, 1931)
    TUR (a)

The Sword of Wotan SEE Sieba

Sylfida SEE La sylphide

Sylfiden SEE La sylphide

Sylfidy SEE Les sylphides

La sylphide (Jean-Madeleine Schneitzhoeffer or Herman
    Lovenskjold, 1832)
    *Syfida; *Sylfiden
    ASC (a,i); BAI (a); BAL; BAM (a,i); BAN; BAO (a); BCB
    (a,i); BRI (a,i); CLA (a,i); CRB (a); DOD (a); GRU
    (a,i); HEA (a,i); KER (a); LAX (a,i); MAY (a!,i); PHA
    (a,i); REB (a); REG (a); REY (a,i); SIM (a,i); TER (a);
    TES (a); TUR (a); VER (a)

Les sylphides (Frédéric Chopin, 1907)
        *Chopiniana; *Shopeniana; *Sylfidy; *The Sylphs;
        *The Wood Nymphs
        ASC (a); BAI (a); BAL (a); BAM (a); BAN; BAO (a); BCB
        (a,i); BRI (a); BRU (i); CLA; CRB (a); CRT (a,i); DAS;
        DET (i!); DOD (i); DRE (i); EWE; GOO (a,i,m); GRU (a,i);
        KOC (x); KRO (i); LAW (a,i,m); LAX (a,i); PHA (a); REB
        (a); REG (a); REY (a,i); REZ (a,b,i); ROB; SEY (x); SIM
        (a); STO (i); TER; TES (a); TUR (a,i); UNT (i); VER (a)

The Sylphs SEE Les sylphides

Sylvia (Léo Delibes, 1876)
        *Diana's Nymph; *Nimfa Diany; *The Nymph of Diana;
        *La Nymphe de Diane; *Die Nymphe der Diana; *Sylwia
        BAI (a); BAL (i); BAM (a); BAN; BBT (a,i); BCB (a,i);
        BET (x); CRB (i); CRC (a,i); DAS; DRE (i,m); EWE; FIS
        (a,i,m!); LAW (m); PHA (a); REG (a); ROS (i); SIM (a);
        STO; TES; TUR (a); VER (a); VIV (a,i); WIN

Sylvia: pas de deux (Léo Delibes, 1950)
    REZ (a,b,i); TER; TES

Sylwia SEE Sylvia

Symfoni i C SEE Le palais de cristal

Symphonic Variations (César Franck, 1946)
    BAL; BAM (a); BAN; BAO (a); BRI (i); CLA; DRE; GRU
    (a,i); TER; TES

Symphonie concertante (Wolfgang Amadeus Mozart, 1947)
    BAL; BAM (a); BAN; DRE (a); LAW (m); REZ (a,b!,i); TER;
    TES

Symphonie fantastique (Hector Berlioz, 1936)
        *An Episode in the Life of an Artist
    BCB (a,i); CRB; DRE (m); GOO (i,m); LAW (i,m!); PHA;
    ROB (a); SEY (x); SIM; TER; TES

La symphonie pour un homme seul (Pierre Schaeffer; Pierre
        Henry, 1955)
        *Symphony for a Lonely Man; *Symphony for a Man
        Alone
    BAM; DRE (a,i); PHA; SIM

Symphony for a Lonely Man SEE La symphonie pour un homme seul

Symphony for a Man Alone SEE La symphonie pour un homme seul

Symphony for Fun (Don Gillis, 1952)
    DRE (a,i)

Symphony in C (Georges Bizet) SEE La palais de cristal

Symphony in C (Igor Stravinsky) SEE Stravinsky: Symphony in C

Symphony in E–Flat (Igor Stravinsky, 1972)
    BAM; REZ (b)

Symphony in Three Movements (Igor Stravinsky, 1972)
    BAM (a); BAO (a); CLA; PHA; REZ (a,b!,i); SIM; TES

Symphony of Psalms SEE Psalmensymfonie

Syn Kaleva SEE Kalevipoeg

Syn marnotrawny SEE Le fils prodigue

Syrena (Witold Maliszewski, 1928)
    TUR (a)

Syrenhaven SEE Jardin aux lilas

De syv Dødssynder SEE Les septs péchés capitaux

Szach–mat SEE Checkmate

Szecherezada SEE Shéhérazade (Nikolai Rimsky–Korsakov)

Il tabacco (Filippo d'Agliè, 1650)
        *Tobacco
    PHA (a); SIM (a)

La table verte SEE Der grüne Tisch

The Tale of the Priest and His Workman Balde (Mikhail
        Chulaki, 1940)
        *The Fairy-tale of the Priest and His Workman
        Balda; *Skazka o pope i rabotnike ego Balde
    BBP (a,i); STO (i)

Les talents lyriques SEE Les fêtes d'hébé

Tales of Hoffmann (Jacques Offenbach, 1972)
    BAM; BAO; CLA (i); TES

Talisman (Riccardo Drigo, 1889)
    BCB; STO

Tally-ho! (Christoph Willibald von Gluck, 1944)
        *The Frail Quarry
    TER; TES

The Taming of the Shrew SEE Die widerspenstigen Zähmung

Tańce polowieckie SEE Danses polovtsiennes

Tangents (Henry Cowell; Lou Harrison, 1968)
    MCD

Tango Chikane (Per Nørgård, after Jacob Gade, 1967)
    TES

Tanťs simfoniiá SEE Dance Symphony

Tänze aus Galanta (Zoltán Kodály, 1954)
    REG (a); WIN

Tarantella (Louis Moreau Gottschalk, 1964)
    BAM (i); BAN; CLA (i); REZ (a,b,i); TES

The Tarantula SEE La tarentule

Taras Bul'ba (Vasilii Solov'ev-Sedoi, 1940)
    BCS (i); STO (i); TES

La tarentule (Casimir Gide, 1839)
        *The Tarantula
    BCB (a,i); PHA (a); SIM (a)

Tatiana (Aleksandr Kreĭn, 1947)
    TES

Taubenflug (Otto-Erich Schilling, 1955)
    REG (a)

Tchaikovsky Concerto No. 2 SEE Ballet Imperial

Tchaikovsky pas de deux (Peter Il'ich Tchaikovsky, 1960)
        *Pas de deux
    BAM (a,i); BAN (i); CLA (i); REZ (a,b,i); TES

Tchaikovsky Suite (Peter Il'ich Tchaikovsky, 1969)
        *Tchaikovsky Suite No. 2; *Tschaikovsky Suite
    BAM (a); BAO (a); REZ (a,b,i); TES

Tchaikovsky Suite No. 1 SEE Reveries

Tchaikovsky Suite No. 2 SEE Tchaikovsky Suite

Tchaikovsky Suite No. 3 SEE Suite No. 3

The Tempest (Arne Nordheim, 1979)
    PHA; SIM

Le temple de la paix (Jean-Baptiste Lully, 1685)
        *The Temple of Peace
    PHA (a); SIM (a)

The Temple of Peace SEE Le temple de la paix

Tempus jazz 67 (Jerzy Milian, 1967)
    TUR (a,i)

Ten (1968)
    MCD (a)

Teni zabytykh predkov (Vitaliĭ Kireĭko, 1960)
    STO

Tent (Alwin Nikolais, 1968)
    MCD (a)

Les tentations de la bergère (Michel Montéclair, 1924)
        *L'amour vainqueur
    DET (x); KOC (x)

Terminal (Herbert Kingsley, 1937)
    BCS (i)

Terrain (Johann Sebastian Bach, 1963)
    MCD (a)

The Test of Love SEE L'épreuve d'amour

Der Teufel im Dorf SEE Davo u selu

Texas Fourth (Harvey Schmidt, 1973)
    BAM

Thamar (Mily Balakirev, 1912)
    BCB (a,i); BRU (i); CRB; DAS; DET (i); DRE; GOO
    (a,i,m); KOC (x); LAW; PHA; SIM

Théa (Cesare Pugni, 1847)
        *La fée aux fleurs; *The Flower Fairy
    BCB; PHA (a,i); SIM (a,i)

Theater (Richard Strauss, 1971)
    *Theatre
    BAM (a); PHA (i); SIM (i); TES

Theatre SEE Theater

Theatre Piece (Wallingford Riegger, 1936)
    MCD (a)

Theme and Variations (Peter Il'ich Tchaikovsky, 1947)
    BAL; BAM; BAN; DRE; GRU (a,i); KRO (i); LAW (i,m); REZ
    (a,b!); TER; TES

Theme and Variations for Piano and Strings SEE The Four
    Temperaments

There Is a Time (Norman Dello Joio, 1956)
    MCD (a); TES

These Three (David Ward-Steinman, 1966)
    TES

The Thief Who Loved a Ghost (Julian Freedman or Carl Maria
    von Weber, 1950)
    BAL; BAN

Thijl Uilenspiegel (Uwe Ködderitzsch, 1965)
    REB (a,i)

Third Symphony SEE Dritte Sinfonie von Gustav Mahler

Third Symphony by Gustav Mahler SEE Dritte Sinfonie von
    Gustav Mahler

This Property is Condemned (Geneviève Pitot, 1957)
    TES

This, That and the Other (Igor Wakhevich, 1977)
  PHA; SIM

The Three-cornered Hat (Manuel de Falla, 1919)
      *Der Dreispitz; *El sombrero de tres picos; *Den
      trekantede hat; *Le tricorne; *Trójkatny kapelusz
  ASC (a); BAI (a); BAL; BAM; BAN; BAO (a); BCB (a,i);
  BRI; BRU (i); CLA (i); CRB (i); CRC (a,i); DAS; DET
  (i); DRE (a,m); GOO (a,i,m); GRU (a,i); KOC (x); LAW
  (a,i!,m); PHA; REB (a); REG (a); ROB (a); SEY (x); SIM;
  STO; TER; TES; TUR (a,i); VER (a); WIN

Three Epitaphs (1960)
  MCD

Three Essays (Charles Ives, 1974)
  BAM

The Three Fat Men (Viktor Oransky, 1935)
      *Tri tolstîaka
  BCB (i); STO

The Three Gifts SEE Kermessen i Brügge

The Three Musketeers SEE De tre musketerer

Three Preludes (Sergei Rachmaninov, 1969)
  TES

The Three Sundays of a Poet SEE The Unicorn, the Gorgon and
      the Manticore

Three Virgins and a Devil (Ottorino Respighi, 1941)
  BAM; BAO (a); DAS; DRE; ROB; TER; TES

Threnody (Benjamin Britten, 1968)
  TES

Thyrsis and Clore SEE Tirsi e Clori

Tiĭna (Lidiĩa Auster, 1955)
    STO

Til Eulenspiegel SEE Till Eulenspiegel

Till Eulenspiegel (Richard Strauss, 1916)
        *Til Eulenspiegel; *Tyl Eulenspiegel; *Tyl
        Ulenspiegel
    BAL (a,i); BAM (a); BAN (i); DRE (a,i); KOC (x); LAW
    (i,m); PHA (a,i); REZ (a,b!,i); SIM (a,i); TER; TES

The Tiller in the Fields (Anton Dvořák, 1979)
    PHA; SIM

Tilt (Igor Stravinsky, 1971)
    BAM

A Time (1968)
    MCD (a)

The Time Before the Time After (Igor Stravinsky, 1972)
        *After the Time Before
    MCD

Time Out of Mind (Paul Creston, 1963)
    BAN; TES

Time Past Summer SEE Time Passed Summer

Time Passed Summer (Peter Il'ich Tchaikovsky, 1974)
        *Time Past Summer
    BAM; TES

Time Table (Aaron Copland, 1941)
     REZ (a,b,i)

Tiresias (Constant Lambert, 1951)
     BAL; BAN; BBT (a,i); CRB (a); DRE (m); TER

Tirsi e Clori (Claudio Monteverdi, 1616)
          *Thyrsis and Clore
     PHA (a); SIM (a)

I Titani (Salvatore Viganò, 1819)
          *The Titans
     BCB (a,i); PHA (a,i); SIM (a,i)

The Titans SEE I Titani

Tobacco SEE Il tabacco

Eine Tochter Kastiliens SEE Daughter of Castille

The Toilet of Venus SEE La toilette de Vénus

La toilette de Vénus (François Granier, 1757)
          *Loves Ruses; *Les ruses de l'amour; *The Toilet
          of Venus
     PHA (a,i); SIM (a,i)

Tolv med posten (Knudåge Riisager, 1942)
          *Twelve by the Mail; *Twelve for the Mail-coach
     BBP (a,i)

Le tombeau de Couperin SEE Vier mal vier

Tommy (Peter D. Townshend, 1970)
     TES

Toreadoren (Edvard Helsted, 1840)
    ASC (a,i)

Tornerose SEE The Sleeping Beauty (Peter Il'ich Tchaikovsky)

Tower (Alwin Nikolais, 1965)
    MCD (a)

The Toybox SEE La bôite à joujoux

Traces (Gustav Mahler, 1973)
    BAM

La tragedia di Orfeo (Wilhelm Killmayer, 1961)
    WIN

Le tragédie di Salomé (Florent Schmitt, 1907)
        *The Tragedy of Salome
    BAI (a); BET; DET (x); LAW (m); PHA; SIM

The Tragedy of Salome SEE Le tragédie de Salomé

Le train bleu (Darius Milhaud, 1924)
        *The Blue Train
    BCB (a,i); DET (x); GOO (a,m); KOC (x); PHA; SIM

The Traitor (Gunther Schuller, 1954)
    TES

Transcendence (Franz Liszt, 1935)
    REZ (a,b,i)

Transit (1969)
    MCD (a)

Trap of Light SEE Piège de lumière

The Traveling Players SEE Les forains

De tre gaver SEE Kermessen i Brügge

De tre musketerer (Georges Delerue, 1966)
        *The Three Musketeers
    TES

Trieze danses (André Grétry, 1948)
    BBT (a,i)

Den trekantede hat SEE The Three-cornered Hat

Trend (Wallingford Riegger; Edgar Varèse, 1937)
    MCD (a)

Tri mushketera (Veniamin Basner, 1964)
    STO (i)

Tri tolstiaka SEE The Three Fat Men

Triad (Sergei Prokofiev, 1972)
    BAM (a); BAO (a); TES (i)

The Trial of Damis SEE Ruses d'amour

Tribute (César Franck, 1963)
    TES

Le tricorne SEE The Three-cornered Hat

Trifles SEE Les petits riens

Trinity (Alan Raph; Lee Holdridge, 1969)
    BAM (a); BAO (a); GRU (a,i); TES (a,i)

Trio (1966)
        *The Mind is a Muscle, Part I
    MCD (a)

Le triomphe de l'amour (Jean-Baptiste Lully, 1681)
        *The Triumph of Love
    BAI (a); PHA (a); SIM (a)

Le triomphe de l'amour (Jañis Medinš, 1935)
    BCS (a)

Le triomphe de Neptune SEE The Triumph of Neptune

I trionfli di Petrarca SEE Per la dolce memoria di quel giorno

Triptych (Meredith Monk, 1973)
    MCD (a)

Tristan (Richard Wagner, 1958)
    TER

Triumf respubliki SEE Plamĩa parizha

The Triumph of Bacchus and Ariadne (Vittorio Rieti, 1948)
    REZ (a,b,i)

Triumph of Death SEE Dødens triumf

The Triumph of Love SEE Le triomphe de l'amour (Jean-
        Baptiste Lully)

The Triumph of Neptune (Lord Berners, 1926)
    *Le triomphe de Neptune
    BCB (a); DAS; DET (x); KOC (x); LAW (m)

The Triumphs of Petrarch SEE Per la dolce memoria di quel
    giorno

Trois valses romantiques (Emmanuel Chabrier, 1967)
    BAM; BAN; REZ (a,b); TES

Trójkatny kapelusz SEE The Three-cornered Hat

Trold kan taemmes SEE Der widerspenstigen Zahmung

Tropoĭu groma SEE The Path of Thunder

Trumpet Concerto (Franz Joseph Haydn, 1950)
    DRE

Tschaikovsky Concerto No. 2 SEE Ballet Imperial

Tschaikovsky Suite SEE Tchaikovsky Suite

Tschaikovsky Suite No. 1 SEE Reveries

TSar'-devit͡sa SEE The Little Humpbacked Horse (Cesare Pugni)

Twelfth Night (Edvard Grieg, 1942)
    DAS

The Twelve (Boris Tishchenko, 1964)
    *Dvenadt͡sat'
    STO (i); TES

Twelve by the Mail SEE Tolv med posten

Twelve for the Mail-coach SEE Tolv med posten

Twice (Herbie Mann; Steven Miller Band; James Brown;
        Santana, 1970)
    BAM

Twilight (John Cage, 1972)
    CLA (i); PHA; SIM

The Two Creoles SEE Les deux créoles

The Two Pigeons SEE Les deux pigeons

The Two Roses (Aleksandr Lensky, 1941)
        *Du-Gul'
    BCS

Tyl Eulenspiegel SEE Till Eulenspiegel

Tyl Ulenspiegel SEE Till Eulenspiegel

Tytanie i Osiol (Zbigniew Turski, 1967)
    TUR (a)

Tzaddik (Aaron Copland, 1974)
    BAM; TES

Tzigane (Maurice Ravel, 1975)
    BAM; REZ (a,b!,i)

The Ultimate Pastorale SEE Ubran Recreation/The Ultimate
        Pastorale

Ulven SEE Le loup

Umierajacy labedź SEE The Dying Swan

Umiraĩushchiĭ lebed SEE The Dying Swan

Umirajusjtjij lebed SEE The Dying Swan

The Unchaperoned Daughter SEE La fille mal gardée

Undertow (William Schuman, 1945)
    BAL; BAM; BAN; BAO; CRB; LAW (a,i,m); ROB (a); TER; TES

Undine (Hans Werner Henze, 1958)
        *Ondine; *Ondyna
        BAM (a); BAN; BRI; CLA (i); REB (a); TES; TUR (a);
        WIN (i)

Undine (Cesare Pugni) SEE Ondine (Cesare Pugni)

Unfinished Symphony (Franz Schubert, 1958)
    BAM (a); BAO (a); TES

Den Unge Mand og Døden SEE Le jeune homme et la mort

The Unicorn, the Gorgon, and the Manticore (Gian Carlo
        Menotti, 1957)
        *The Three Sundays of a Poet
    PHA; REZ (a,b,i); SIM; TER; TES

Union Jack (Hershy Kay, 1976)
    BAM (a,i); CLA (i); REZ (a!,b!,i)

Union Pacific (Nicolas Nabokov, 1934)
    BCB (a,i); BRU (i); CRB; DET (i); GOO (i,m); ROB (a);
    TER; TES

Untitled (Robert Dennis, 1975)
    GRU (a,i)

Gli uomini di Prometeo SEE Die Geschöpfe des Prometheus

Urban Recreation/The Ultimate Pastorale (1971)
        *The Ultimate Pastorale
    MCD (a)

Useless Precautions SEE La fille mal gardée

Utrachennye illiuzii SEE Lost Illusions

Vaaren (Edvard Grieg, 1942)
        *Le printemps; *Varen
    BBP (a,i)

The Vagabonds (John Ireland, 1946)
    CRB

Vagaries of the Human Heart SEE Les intermittences du coeur

Les vainqueurs (Richard Wagner and classical Indo-Tibetan
        composers, 1969)
    BAM (a); TES

Valentine (Jacob Druckman, 1971)
    BAM; TES

La valse (Maurice Ravel, 1929)
        *Walc; *The Waltz; *Der Walzer
    BAI (a); BAL (a,i); BAM; BAN; BCB; CLA; DRE (a); KRO;
    LAW (m); PHA; REB (a); REG (a); REZ (a,b!,i); SIM; TER;

TES; TUR (a); WIN

Valse fantaisie (Mikhail Glinka, 1953)
REZ (b,i); TER; TES

Valse fantaisie (Mikhail Glinka, 1967) SEE Glinkiana

Valses nobles et sentimentales SEE Adélaïde

Valses et variations SEE Raymonda Variations

Vanina Vanini (Nikolai Karetnikov, 1962)
STO

Varen SEE Vaaren

Variations (Ludwig van Beethoven)
DET (x)

Variations (Igor Stravinsky, 1966)
BAM; BAN; REZ (a,b!,i)

Variations V (John Cage, 1965)
MCD (a)

Variations for Four (Marguerite Keogh, 1957)
BAM (a); TER; TES

Variations from "Don Sebastian" (Gaetano Donizetti, 1960)
    *Donizetti Variations
BAM; BAN; REZ (a,b!,i); TES

Variations on Euclid (1933)
SEY (x)

Variations pour une port et un soupir (Pierre Henry, 1974)
    BAM (a); REZ (a,b,i); TES (a,i)

Variegations (1958)
    MCD (a)

Vendetta SEE Revanche

Venetian Festival SEE Les fêtes venitiennes

Veneziana (Gaetano Donizetti, 1953)
    BBT (a,i); DRE

La ventana (Hans Christian Lumbye; Wilhelm Christian Holm,
        1854)
    ASC (a,i); CLA (i); TER

Vergebliche Vorsicht SEE La fille mal gardée

Verklungene Feste (François Couperin; Richard Strauss, 1941)
        *Couperin-Suite
    REG (a,i)

Der verlorene Sohn (Hugo Alfvén) SEE Den Förlorade sonen

Der verlorene sohn (Segei Prokoviev) SEE Le fils prodigue

Vert-vert (Édouard Deldevez; Jean Tolbecque, 1851)
    BCB (a)

Vesna sviashchennaia SEE Le sacre du printemps

The Vestal Virgin SEE La vestale

La **vestale** (Salvatore Viganò, 1818)
        *The Vestal Virgin
    BCB (a,i); PHA (a); SIM (a)

Vestris (Gennadi Banschikov, 1969)
    BAM

Vienna 1814 (Carl Maria von Weber, 1940)
    BCS: SEY (x)

Vienna Waltzes (Johann Strauss; Franz Lehár; Richard
        Strauss, 1977)
    CLA (i); GRU (a,i)

Vier letzte Lieder SEE Four Last songs

Vier mal vier (Maurice Ravel, 1955)
        *La tombeau de Couperin
    BAM; CLA (i); LAW (m); REG (a); REZ (a,b,i)

Die vier temperamente SEE The Four Temperaments

Les vierges folles (Kurt Atterberg, 1920)
    BCB

Vieux souvenirs (1848)
        *La lanterne magique; *The Magic Lantern; *Old
        Memories
    BCS

Viktorka (Zbyněk Vostřák, 1950)
    REB (a)

Vilia SEE The Merry Widow

Villon (Robert Starer, 1966)
      TES (i)

Vindzorskie prokaznitsy SEE The Merry Wives of Windsor

Violin Concerto (Igor Stravinsky, 1972)
      *Stravinsky Violin Concerto
      BAM (a); BAO (a); CLA (i); REZ (a,b,i); TES (i)

Violin Concerto in D SEE Concerto (Peter Il'ich Tchaikovsky)

Le violon du diable (Cesare Pugni, 1849)
      *The Devil's Violin
      BCB (a,i); PHA (a,i); SIM (a,i)

Vision of Marguerite (Franz Liszt, 1952)
      DRE (a)

Vision of Salomé (1907)
      MCD (a,i)

Viva Vivaldi! (Antonio Vivaldi, 1965)
      BAM; BAN; CLA

La vivandière (Cesare Pugni, 1844)
      BCB (a,i); PHA (a); SIM (a)

The Vixen's Choice SEE The Chase

Voices of Spring (Johann Strauss; Mois Zlatin, 1938)
      ROB (a)

Volshebnaia fleĭta SEE The Magic Flute

Voluntaries (Francis Poulenc, 1973)
    ASC (a,i); BAM; CLA (i); GRU (a,i); PHA; SIM

Vremena goda SEE The Seasons (Alexander Glazunov)

Vstrecha (Dimitri Shostakovich, 1962)
    STO

The Wail (John Cage, 1969)
    MCD (a)

Walc SEE La valse

Walk to the Paradise Garden (Frederick Delius, 1972)
    BAM (i)

The Walnut Tree of Benevento SEE Il noce di Benevento

Walpurgis Night (Charles Gounod, 1941)
    BAM; BAN; TES (a,i)

Walt Whitman Suite (Genèvieve Pitot, 1934)
    MCD (a)

The Waltz (Maurice Ravel) SEE La valse

Waltz (Johann Strauss, 1973)
    MCD (a)

Waltz Academy (Vittorio Rieti, 1944)
    LAW (i,m); ROB (a)

Waltz-Scherzo (Peter Il'ich Tchaikovsky, 1958)
    REZ (a,b); TER

Der Walzer SEE La valse

The Wanderer (Franz Schubert, 1941)
    DAS

Wariacje 4 : 4 (Franciszek Wózniak, 1966)
    TUR (a,i)

Water Study (1928)
    MCD (a); TES

Waterman Switch (Giuseppe Verdi, 1965)
    MCD (a)

Watermill (Teiji Ito, 1972)
    BAM (a); BAO (a); REZ (a,b!,i); TES

The Wayward Daughter SEE La fille mal gardée

The Wedding (1961)
    MCD (a)

The Wedding (Igor Stravinsky) SEE Les noces

A Wedding Bouquet (Lord Berners, 1937)
    BAL; BAM; BAN; BRI; CLA (i); CRB; DRE (a); TER; TES

The Wedding Breakfast at the Eiffel Tower SEE Les mariés de
    la Tour Eiffel

The Wedding of the Gods SEE Le nozze degli dei

A Wedding Present (Béla Bartók, 1962)
    BRI

Wednesday Class (1973)
    TES

Weewis (Stanley Walden, 1971)
    BAM; TES

Der weisse Rose (Wolfgang Fortner, 1951)
    REG (a); WIN

Wesele SEE Les noces

Wesele w Ojcowie (Karol Kurpiński, 1823)
    TUR (a,i)

Wesole miasteczko (Stefan Kisielewski, 1967)
    TUR (a)

Western Symphony (Hershy Kay, 1954)
    BAM (a); BAN; KRO; PHA (i); REZ (a,b!,i); SIM (i); TER;
    TES

What Love Tells Me SEE Ce que l'amour me dit

The Whims of Cupid SEE Amors og balletmesterens luner

The Whims of Cupid and the Ballet Master SEE Amors og
    balletmesterens luner

White Jade (Clifford Vaughan, 1926)
    SHE (a,i)

Whitip (1971)
    MCD (a)

Who Cares? (George Gershwin, 1970)
    BAM (a!,i); BAO (a!); CLA (i); REZ (a,b!,i); TES (i)

Les whoops–de–doo (Don Gillis, 1959)
    TES (i)

Der widerspenstigen Zähmung (Kurt–Heinz Stolz, after
        Domenico Scarlatti, 1969)
        *The Taming of the Shrew; *Trold kan taemmes
    ASC (a); BAM; BAO; BRI (i); CLA (i); GRU (a,i); PHA
    (i); SIM (i); TES (i)

The Widow in the Mirror SEE Enken i spejlet

Wierchy (Artur Malawski, 1962)
    TUR (a)

Die Wilis SEE Giselle

Les Wilis SEE Giselle

Will o' the Wisp (Virgil Thomson, 1953)
    REZ (a,b)

William Tell Variations (Gioacchino Rossini, 1969)
    BAM; TES

The Wind in the Mountains (Laurence Rosenthal, 1965)
    BAM; TES

Windsong (Edward Elgar, 1969)
    TES

Winesburg Portraits (1963)
    MCD (a)

Winter Night (Sergei Rachmaninov, 1948)
    BBT (a,i); DRE

Winterbranch (La Monte Young, 1964)
    MCD (a)

Winter's Eve (Benjamin Britten, 1957)
    TER

The Wise and Foolish Virgins SEE The Wise Virgins

The Wise Virgins (Johann Sebastian Bach, 1940)
        *The Wise and Foolish Virgins
    CRB; DAS; DRE; EWE; LAW

The Witch (Maurice Ravel, 1950)
    REZ (a,b)

The Witch Boy (Leonard Salzedo, 1956)
    BAM (a); BRI

With My Red Fires (Wallingford Riegger, 1936)
    MCD (a)

Within the Quota (Cole Porter, 1923)
    BCB

The Wolf SEE Le loup

The Wood Nymphs SEE Les Sylphides

The Woodcut Prince SEE The Wooden Prince

The Wooden Prince (Béla Bartók, 1917)
        *Drewniany ksiaze; *A fából faragott királyfi;

*Der holzgeschnitzte Prinz; *The Woodcut Prince
REB (a,i); REG (a,i); STO; TUR (a,i)

The Would-be Gentleman (Jean-Baptiste Lully) SEE Le
bourgeois gentilhomme (Jean-Baptiste Lully)

The Would-be Gentleman (Richard Strauss) SEE Le bourgeois
gentilhomme (Richard Strauss)

Would They or Wouldn't They? (1963)
MCD

Der wundernbare Mandarin (Béla Bartók, 1926)
*A csodálatos mandarin; *Cudowny mandaryn; *Den
forunderlige mandarin; *Il mandarino meraviglioso;
*The Miraculous Mandarin
ASC (a); BAL; BAN; DRE (a); PHA (i); REB (a); REG
(a,i); REZ (a,b,i); STO; SIM (i); TER; TES; TUR (a,i)

X Land (Barre Phillips; John Surman; Dieter Feichtner, 1975)
PHA; SIM

Yankee Clipper (Paul Bowles, 1937)
BCS (i); REZ (a,b,i)

Yedda (Olivier Métra, 1879)
BCB (a,i)

The Yogi (Walter Meyrowitz, 1908)
MCD (a)

The Young Lady and the Hooligan (Dimitri Shostakovich, 1962)
*Baryshnîa i khuligan; *The Lady and the Hooligan;
*Das Mädchen und der Rowdy
REB (a); STO (i); TES

The Young Man and Death SEE Le Jeune homme et la mort

Youth (Mikhail Chulaki, 1949)
        *IUnost'
    STO (i); TES

Z chlopa krol (Grażyna Bacewicz, 1954)
    TUR(a)

Zaczarowana oberża (Antoni Szalowski, 1962)
    TUR (a,i)

Der Zauberladen SEE La boutique fantasque

Zéphire et Flore (Vladimir Dukelsky, 1925)
        *Zephyr and Flora
    DAS; DET (i); KOC (x)

Zephyr and Flora SEE Zéphire et Flore

Der zerbrochene Krug (Rudolf Wagner-Régeny, 1937)
    REB (a)

Zhanna d'Ark SEE Joan of Arc

Zhar-ptitsa SEE L'oiseau de feu

Zielony stól SEE Der grüne Tisch

Ziggurat (Karlheinz Stockhausen, 1967)
    BRI

Zlota Kaczka (Jan Adam Maklakiewicz, 1951)
    TUR (a)

Zloty wiek SEE The Golden Age

Zodiac (Rudolf Revil, 1947)
    REZ (a,b,i)

Zolotoĭ petushok SEE Le coq d'or

Zolotoĭ vek SEE The Golden Age

Zolushka SEE Cinderella (Sergei Prokofiev)

Zoraiīa SEE Zoraiya

Zoraiya (Léon Minkus, 1881)
        *The Moorish Woman in Spain; *Zoraiīa
    BCB

Zvezdy SEE The Stars

Zwei fanden den Weg (Wolfgang Hudy, 1960)
    REB (a)

COMPOSER INDEX

Unknown authorship, diverse authorship, or no music:
Acapulco; Accumulation, Primary Accumulation, Group
Accumulation; After "Suite"; Anonymous; Ballet de la
prospérité des armes de France; Ballet des échecs;
Carnation; Celebration; Cesare in Egitto; Choreographic
Minatures; Circo de España; Il convalescente
innamorato; Il corsaro; Countdown; Country Houses;
Coverage; Le création; Cuadro flamenco; Dance; Dancing
with Maisie Paradocks; A Dream under a Black Hat; Duet
with Cat's Scream and Locomotive; Electra; Es mujer;
Fanga; La fille mal gardée; Fire Dance; Folksay; Forces
of Rhythm; Forevermore; Games; Generation; Grandstand;
Half-time; Heads; Héliogabale; Heretic; Hindu Serenade;
Hoopla; How to Pass, Kick, Fall and Run; L'indifferent;
Jazz Concert; Junk Dances; Leadville; A Legend of Rama;
Light; Lot Piece Day/Night; The Maske of Beauty; Meat
Joy; Medley; Memory; Monkshood's Farewell; Moves; Mr.
Puppet; Narcissus Rising; Nautch; Negro Spirituals;
Notebook; Obbligato '69 N.Y.; October Parade; The One
Hundreds; Otello; Panamerica; Passin' Through;
Pelican; Physical Things; Poppy; Psyché et l'amour;
Quilt, Revised; Rainbow 'Round My Shoulder; Random
Breakfast; Re-moves; The Red Detachment of Women;
Revelations; Il ritorno di Agamennone; Rocks; Roof
Piece; Route 6; Saint George and the Dragon; Satisfyin'
Lover; Sephardic Songs; The Shakers; Signals II; 16
Millimeter Earrings; Songs for Young Lovers; Soweto;
Gli Strelizzi; Ten; Three Epitaphs; A Time; Transit;
Trio A; Urban Recreation/The Ultimate Pastorale;
Variations on Euclid; Variegations; Vieux souvenirs;
Vision of Salomé; The Wedding; Wednesday Class; Whitip;
Winesburg Portraits; Would They or Wouldn't They?

Adam, Adolphe (1803-1856). Beatrice di Gand; Le corsaire;
Le corsaire pas de deux; Le diable à quatre; La fille
du Danube; La filleule des fées; Giselle; Giselle's
Revenge; La jolie fille de Gand; Katerina; The Marble
Maiden
Addison, John (1920-   ). Carte blanche
Agliè, Filippo d' (1604-1667). Ballet des montagnards; Il
gridelino; Il tabacco
Alcantara, Burt. Journal; Nostalgia
Alfvén, Hugo (1872-1960). Den förlorade sonen; La nuit de
Saint-Joan
Alpert, Herb (1935-   ). The Closer She Gets...The Better
She Looks
Anderson, Pasquita. Blues Suite; Rites de passage

Andriessen, Juriaan (1925-   ). Jones Beach
Angiolini, Gasparo (1731-1803). Le départ d'Enée; La morte
    di Cleopatra
Antheil, George (1900-1959). Capitol of the World
Applebaum, Stan (1922-   ). PAMTGG
ApIvor, Denis (1916-   ). Blood Wedding; A Mirror for
    Witches; Saudades
Appleton, Jon H. (1939-   ). Anaendrom
Archilei, Antonio (1550-1612). La pellegrina
Arends, Andrei. Salammbô
Arensky, Anton (1861-1906). Cléopâtre; Les orientales
Arlen, Harold (1905-   ). Once More, Frank
Armsheimer, Johann. Cavalry Halt
Arnell, Richard (1917-   ). The Great Detective;
    Harlequin in April; Punch and the Child
Arnold, Malcolm (1921-   ). Homage to the Queen; Rinaldo
    and Armida; Solitaire
Arrieu, Claude (1903-   ). La commedia umana
Arrigo, Girolamo (1930-   ). L'or des fous
Asaf'ev, Boris (1884-1949). Christmas Eve; The Flames of
    Paris; The Fountain of Bakhchisarai; Lost Illusions;
    Partisan Days; The Prisoner of the Caucasus
Atterberg, Kurt (1887-1974). Les vierges
Auber, Daniel (1782-1871). Le dieu et al bayadère; La
    Gitana; Grand pas classique; Marco Spada; Quelques
    fleurs; Les rendez-vous
Auger, Paul. La douairiére de Billebahaut
Auric, Georges (1899-1983). La concurrence; Les fâcheux; La
    guirlande de Campra; Les mariés de la Tour Eiffel; Les
    matelots; La pastorale; Phèdre
Auster, Lidiia (1912-   ). Tiina

Bacewicz, Grazyna (1909-1969). Esik w Ostendzie; Z chlopa
    krol
Bach, Johann Sebastian (1685-1750). Actus tragicus; Aimez-
    vous Bach?; Air and Variations; Bach Sonata; Beggar's
    Dance; Brandenburg Nos. 2 and 4; Concerto barocco;
    Courante; Double Concerto; Les éléments; Esplanade;
    Étude; The Goldberg Variations; In Nightly Revels; Le
    jeune homme et la mort; Junction; The Night and
    Silence; Notre Faust; Offrande choreographique; Opus
    Lamaître; Passacaglia and Fugue in C Minor; Recital for
    Cello and Eight Dancers; Terrain; The Wise Virgins
Badalbeili, Afrasiiab (1907-   ). The Maiden's Tower
Badings, Henk (1907-   ). Jungle; Metallics
Baigliù. Achille in Sciro

Baillou, Louis de (1735-1809). Apollo placato; La prima età
     dell'innocenza
Baird, Tadeusz (1928-   ). Cztery eseje
Bajetti, Giovanni (1815-1876). Les éléments; Faust
Balanchivadze, Andrei (1906-   ). The Heart of the Hills
Balakirev, Mily (1837-1910). Thamar
Balasanian, Sergei (1902-   ). Leila and Medzhun;
     Shakuntala
Ballard, Louis (1931-   ). Four Moons
Banfield, Raffaello de (1922-   ). Le combat
Banschikov, Gennadi (1943-   ). Vestris
Baranović, Krešimir (1894-1975). Licitarsko srce
Barber, Samuel (1910-1981). Capricorn concerto; Cave of the
     Heart; La damnée; Souvenirs
Bardi, Giovanni (1534-1612). La pellegrina
Bartók, Béla (1881-1945). Bartók Concerto; Bartók No. 3;
     Caprichos; Home; Hungarica; Journey; Medea; Night City;
     Opus 12; The Prisoners; Rituals; Sonate à trois; A
     Wedding Present; The Wooden Prince; Der wunderbare
     Mandarin
Baschet, Bernard (1917-   ). Huescape
Basner, Veniamin (1925-   ). Tri mushketera
Bataille, Gabriel (1575-1630). Ballet de la délivrance de
     Renaud
Bate, Stanley (1913-1959). Highland Fling
Bax, Arnold (1883-1953). Picnic at Tintagel
Bayer, Joseph (1852-1913). Die Puppenfee
The Beach Boys. Duece coupe
The Beatles. Mods and Rockers
Beauchamp, Pierre (1636-1705). Les fâcheux
Beaulieu, Lambert de (fl. c1576-1590). Ballet comique de la
     Reine
Bechet, Sidney (1897-1959). District Storyville
Beethoven, Ludwig van (1770-1827). Adagio Hammerklavier;
     Dance Symphony; Four Bagatelles; Die Geschöpfe des
     Prometheus; La gloire; Grosse fuge; L'île des pirates;
     Les intermittences du coeur; Neuvième symphonie; Orbs;
     Piece Period; Prometeo; La septième symphonie; Variations
Beiderbecke, Bix (1903-1931). The Bix Pieces
Belafonte, Harry (1927-   ). Blues for the Jungle
Bellini, Vincenzo (1801-1835). Night Shadow; Romantic Age
Bennett, Richard Rodney (1936-   ). Isadora; Jazz Calendar
Benoist, François (1794-1878). Le diable amoureaux; La
     gypsy; Paquerette
Bentzoon, Niels Viggo (1919-   ). Kurtisanen
Berg, Alban (1885-1935). Lyric Suite
Berger, Theodor (1905-   ). Homerische Symphonie

Britten, Benjamin (1913-1976). Fanfare; Haus der Schatten;
    Illuminations; Die im Schatten leben; Jinx; The Prince
    of the Pagodas; Sea Change; Simple Symphony; Threnody;
    Winter's Eve
Brown, James. Twice
Brown, Oscar, Jr. (1926-   ). Blues for the Jungle
Bruneau, Alfred (1857-1934). Les bacchantes
Bruns, Viktor (1904-   ). Neue Odyssee; Das Recht de Herrn
Bucchi, Valentino (1916-1976). Laudes evangelii
Burghauser, Jarmil (1921-   ). Diener zweier Herren
Burgmüller, Friedrich (1806-1874). La péri
Burgon, Geoffry (1941-   ). Songs, Lamentations and
    Praises
Byng, George W. Femina
Byrd, William (1543-1623). Prologue

Caccini, Giulio (1545-1618). La pellegrina
Cage, John (1912-   ). Aeon; Antic Meet; The Seasons; Solo
    for Voice I; Suite for Five in Space and Time;
    Twilight; Variations V; The Wail
Cambefort, Jean de (1605-1661). Le ballet royal de la nuit
Campra, André (1660-1744). L'Europa galante; Les fêtes
    Venitiennes; La guirlande de Campra
Caraffa, Michele (1787-1872). Der Schweizer Milchmädchen
Carlini, Luigi. L'île des pirates
Carpenter, John Alden (1876-1951). Raggedy Ann and Raggedy
    Andy; Skyscrapers
Carter, Elliott (1908-   ). The Minotaur; Pocahontas
Casella, Alfredo (1883-1947). Les comédiens jaloux; La
    giara
Cavalieri, Emilio de (1550-1602). La pellegrina
Cavos, Caterino (1776-1840). Il prigioniero del Caucaso;
    Raoul de Créquis
Chabrier, Emmanuel (1841-1894). Ballabile; Bar aux Folies-
    Bergère; Bourrée fantasque; Chabriesque; Cortège
    burlesque; Cortège parisien; Cotillon; Folk Dance;
    Foyer de la danse; Trois valses romantiques
Chailley, Jacques (1910-   ). Die Dame und das
    Einhorn
Chailley, Luciano (1920-   ). Fantasmi al Grand Hotel
Chapí y Lorente, Ruperto (1851-1909). Fanfarita
Chausson, Ernest (1855-1899). Jardin aux lilas; Paean
Chavchavadzé, Georges (1904-1962). L'aigrette
Chávez, Carlos (1899-1978). Canto indio; Dark Meadow; H. P.
Cherubini, Luigi (1760-1842). Achille à Scyros
Chitti, Giovanni. Pietro Micca

The Gods Amused; Greek Dreams with Flute; Île des
  sirènes; Jeux; Once Upon a Time; Printemps; Protée;
  Sarabande and Danse (I); Sarabande and Danse (II); The
  Still Point
Deldevez, Édouard (1817-1897). Paquita; Vert-vert
Deleru, Georges (1925-   ). Enetime; De tre musketerer
Delibes, Leo (1836-1891). Cobras; Coppélia; Fadetta; Pas de
  Deux and Divertissement; Radha; Soir de fête; La
  source; Sylvia; Sylvia: pas de deux
Delius, Frederick (1862-1934). Nocturne; Romeo and Juliet;
  Walk to the Paradise Garden
Dello Joio, Norman (1913-   ). Diversion of Angels; On
  Stage!; Seraphic Dialogue; There is a Time
Delmuth, Norman. Planetomania
Delvincourt, Claude (1888-1954). Lucifer
Dennis, Robert (1933-   ). Untitled
d'Erlanger Frédéric SEE Erlanger, Frédéric, d'
Diamond, David (1915-   ). Classic Kite Tails
Diego, Emilio de. Bodas de sangre
Dieckmann, Carl-Heinz (1923-   ). Kreuzbauer Ulrike
Dlugoszewski, Lucia (1931-   ). 8 Clear Places; Here and
  Now with Watchers
Dohnányi, Ernö (1877-1960). The Five Gifts; The Holy Torch;
  The Shadow
Donizetti, Gaetano (1797-1848). Danza a quattro; Variations
  from "Don Sebastian"; Veneziana
Dowland, John (1563-1626). The Consort
Downes, Bob. Blind-sight; Stages
Drigo, Riccardo (1846-1930). The Beautiful Pearl; Le
  corsaire pas de deux; Harlequinade; Harlequinade pas de
  deux; The Magic Flute; Talisman
Druckman, Jacob (1928-   ). Valentine
Dukas, Paul (1865-1935). La péri
Dukelsky, Vladimir (1903-1969). Jardin public; Zéphire et
  Flore
Duplessis, Paul. Hip and Straight
Dupuy, Edouard (1770-1822). Fjernt fra Danmark
Durondeau, Henri. Acis et Galathée
Durondeau, Jean. Les deux créoles
Dutilleux, Henri (1916-   ). La belle au bois dormant; Le
  loup
Dvořák, Antonin (1841-1904). The Leaves are Fading; The
  Tiller in the Fields

Egk, Werner (1901-   ). Abraxas; Die chinesische
  Nachtigall; Französische Suite; Joan von Zarissa; Ein
  Sommertag

Einem, Gottfried von (1918–   ). Prinzessin Turandot; Rondo
    vom goldenen Kalb
El-Dabh, Halim (1921–   ). Clytemnestra
Elgar, Edward (1857–1934). Amoras; Enigma Variations;
    Windsong
Ellington, Duke (1899–1974). Congo Tango Palace; District
    Storyville; Pas de Duke; The River; Road of the Pheobe
    Snow
Erlanger, Frédéric, d' (1868–1943). Les cents baisers;
    Cinderella
Eshpai, Andrei (1925–   ). The Angara
Evans, Gil (1912–   ). Congo Tango Palace
Evlakhov, Orest (1912–1973). Ivushka

Falla, Manuel de (1876–1946). El amor brujo; The Soldier
    and the Gypsy; The Three-cornered Hat
Fariñas, Carlos (1934–   ). Despertar
Farkas, Ferenc (1905–   ). Mischievous Students
Farnaby, Giles (1563–1640). Prologue
Fauré, Gabriel (1845–1924). Black and White and Sparkle
    Plenty; Fadette; La fête étrange; Jewels; Malédictions
    et lumières; Les meninãs; Pelléas et Mélisande
Favart, Charles Simon (1710–1792). La chercheuse d'esprit
Feichtner, Dieter. X Land
Feĭgin, Leonid. Don-Zhuan
Feldman, Morton (1926–   ). Figure of Memory; Summerspace
Ferchen, Tim. Changing Pattern Steady Pulse
Fere, Vladimir (1902–1971). Anar
Fernando. Bleecker to West 80th and Epilogue
Field, John (1782–1837). Pas des déesses
Fine, Vivian (1913–   ). Opus 51
Firbank. The Loves of Mars and Venus
Firtich, G. The Bedbug
Forest, Jean Kurt (1909–1975). Sadako
Forti, Simone (1935–   ). Planes
Fortner, Wolfgang (1907–   ). Der weisse Rose
Foss, Lukas (1922–   ). Gift of the Magi
Foster, Stephen (1826–1864). Blackface; Drums, Dreams and
    Banjos; A Polite Entertainment for Ladies and Gentlemen
Fountain, Primous, III (1903–   ). Manifestations
Françaix, Jean (1912–   ). À la françaix; Beach;
    Clockwise; Concertino; La dame à la lune; Les
    demoiselles de la nuit; Le roi nu
Franck, César (1822–1870). L'amour et son amour; Symphonic
    Variations; Tribute
Freedman, Harry (1922–   ). Rose Latulippe; The Shining
    People of Leonard Cohen

Freedman, Julian. The Thief Who Loved a Ghost
Freitag, Dorothea (1914-   ). District Storyville
Frescobaldi, Girolamo (1583-1643). Moyen age
Fukushima, Kazuo (1930-   ). Hi-kyồ
Fuleihan, Anis (1901-1970). Mevlevi Dervish

Gabrielli, Nicolò (1814-1891). Les elfes; Gemma
Gade, Jacob (1879-1963). Tango Chikane
Gade, Niels V. (1817-1890). Et folkesagn; Napoli
Gagliano, Marco da (1587-1643). Ballo di donne turche
Gagliano, Vadico. Choros
Gagne, David. After Corinth
Gassmann, Remi. Billy Sunday; Electronics
Gaubert, Phillippe (1879-1941). Alexandre le grande; Le
    chevalier et la damoiselle
Geissler, Fritz (1921-   ). Pigment
Gerhard, Roberto (1896-1970). Don Quixote; Pandora
Gershwin, George (1898-1937). The New Yorker; The Real
    McCoy; Rhapsody in Blue; Who Cares?
Gesualdo, Carlo (1561-1613). Monumentum pro Gesualdo
Gianella, Luigi (1778?-1817). Acis et Galathée
Gide, Casimir (1804-1868). Le diable boiteux; L'île des
    pirates; Ozaï; La tarentule
Gilbert, Ralph. Dreams
Gillet, Ernest (1856-1940). Serpentine
Gillis, Don (1912-1978). Symphony for Fun; Les whoops-de-
    doo
Ginastera, Alberto (1916-   ). Cantata; Ceremonials
Giorza, Paolo (1832-1914). Cleopatra; Shakespeare
Glaser, Franz Joseph (1798-1861). Fjernt fra Danmark
Glaser, G. J. M. The Débutante
Glazunov, Alexander (1865-1936). Ballet School; Birthday
    Offering; Cléopâtre; Cortège hongrois; The Dance Dream; Le
    festin; Grand pas-Glazounov; Les orientales; Pas de
    dix; Raymonda; Raymonda Variations; Ruses d'amour; The
    Seasons; Stenka Razine
Glière, Reinhold (1875-1956). The Bronze Horseman,
    Daughter of Castille; The Red Poppy
Glinka, Mikhail (1804-1857). Cléopâtra; Danse brillante; Le
    festin; Glinkiana; Mazurka from "A Life for the Tsar";
    Pas de trois; Valse fantaisie
Gluck, Christoph Willibald von (1714-1787). Chaconne; Don
    Juan (1761); Don Juan (1972); Iphigenia in Aulis; A
    Masque of Beauty and the Shepherd; L'orphelin de la
    Chine; Orpheus and Eurydice; Semiramide; Tally-ho!
Godard, Benjamin (1849-1895). Death of Adonis; Reminiscence
Goldschmidt, Berthold (1903-   ). Chronica

Goldstein, Malcolm (1936–   ). Duet for One Person
Goleminov, Marin (1908–   ). Nestinarka
Gordon, Gavin (1901–   ). The Rake's Progress
Gordon, Kelly (1932–   ). Once More, Frank
Gottschalk, Louis Moreau (1829–1869). Barn Dance; Cakewalk;
    The Fall of a Leaf; Fjernt fra Danmark; Tarantella
Gould, Morton (1913–   ). Clarienade; Fall River Legend;
    Interplay; Jive; The Rehearsal; The Rib of Eve
Gounod, Charles (1818–1893). Cirque de deaux; Gounod
    Symphony; Homage au Ballet; Walpurgis Night
Granados, Enrique (1867–1916). Del amor y de la muerte;
    Goyescas
Granier, François (1717–1779). La toilette de Vénus
Green, Ray (1909–   ). Suspension
Grétry, André (1741–1813). Treize danses
Grieg, Edvard (1843–1907). Concerto; Holberg Suite; The Ice
    Maiden; Les orientales; Twelfth Night; Vaaren
Griesbach, Karl-Rudi (1916–   ). Kleider machen Leute;
    Schneewittchen
Grinblat, Romual'd (1930–   ). Rigonda
Grofe, Ferde (1892–1972). Café society
Guédron, Pierre (1570?–1619?). Ballet de la délivrance de
    Renaud
Guion, David (1892–1981). Barn Dance
Gurst, Lee. Percussion for Six-men; Percussion for Six-
    women
Gyrowetz, Adalbert (1763–1850). Les pages du Duc de
    Vendôme; Der Schweizer Milchmädchen

Hahn, Reynaldo (1875–1947). Le dieu bleu; La fête chez
    Thérèse
Haieff, Alexei (1914–   ). Divertimento
Halvorsen, Johan (1864–1935). Badinage
Hamilton, Judith. The Beloved
Handel, George Frederick (1685–1759). Aureole; Blow-out;
    Concerto grosso; The Figure in the Carpet; The Gods Go
    A-begging; The Great Elopement; Masque of Comus; The
    Origin of Design
Hanuš, Jan (1915–   ). Othello
Haring, Lee. From 1 to 10 to 7
Harman, Carter (1918–   ). Blackface
Harrison, Lou (1917–   ). Gamelan; Tangents
Harsànyi, Tibor (1954–   ). Chota Roustaveli
Hartmann, Johan P. (1805–1900). Et folkesagn
Hartmann, Thomas (1885–1956). The Blood-red Flower
Haufrecht, Herbert (1909–   ). And Daddy was a Fireman
Haydn, Franz Joseph (1732–1809). As Time Goes By; Haydn

Concerto; Meadowlark; Piece Period; Promenade;
    Prometeo; Push Comes to Shove; Trumpet Concerto
Heiss, Hermann (1897-1966). Der Manager
Helsted, Edvard. Blomsterfesten i Genzano; Napoli;
    Toreadoren
Henry, Pierre (1927-   ). Collage III; Huescape; Messe
    pour le temp présent; Nijinsky, clown de Dieu; La
    symphonie pour un homme seul; Variations pour une port
    et un soupir
Henze, Hans Werner (1926-   ). Gemini; Der Idiot; Jack
    Pudding; Undine
Herbert, Victor (1859-1924). At the Cafe Fleurette
Hérold, Louis (1791-1833). La belle au bois dormant; La
    fille mal gardée; La somnambule
Hertel, Peter Ludwig (1817-1899). La fille mal gardée; Flik
    e Flok
Hindemith, Paul (1895-1963). Der Dämon; The Four
    Temperaments; Kammermusik No. 2; Metamorphoses;
    Nobilissima visione; Sinfonietta
Hobson, Michael. Common Ground
Hohensee, Wolfgang. Drosselbart; Sklaven
Hoiby, Lee (1926-   ). After Eden
Holder, Geoffrey (1930-   ). Dougla
Holdridge, Lee (1944-   ). Trinity
Holm, William Christian. Livjaegerne på Amager; La ventana
Honegger, Arthur (1892-1955). Chota Roustaveli; La
    guirlande de Campra; Jeanne au bûcher; Lady into Fox;
    Les mariés de la Tour Eiffel; Skating Rink
Hopkins, Anthony (1921-   ). Café des sports
Hopkins, Kenyon. Rooms
Horowitz, Joseph (1926-   ). Alice in Wonderland
Horst, Louis (1884-1964). Frontier; Primitive Mysteries
Horton, Lester. Salome
Hovhaness, Alan (1911-   ). Greek Dreams with Flute;
    Meditations of Orpheus; Night Song; A Rose for Miss
    Emily; Shirah
Hristić, Stevan (1885-1958). Ohridska legenda
Hubeau, Jean (1917-   ). La fiancée du diable
Hudy, Wolfgang. Das kalte Herz; Die lachende Maske; Zwei
    fanden den Weg
Hunger, Hans Helmut. Frauen unserer Tage
Husa, Karel (1921-   ). Ontogeny

I͡Arullin, Farid. Schuraleh
Ibert, Jacques (1890-1962). Les amours de Jupiter; La
    ballade de la géole de Reading; Le chevalier errant;
    Impromptu au bois; Misalliance; Street Games

Lifar, Serge (1905-1986). David triomphant; Icare
Ligeti, György (1923-   ). Epitaph
Lincke, Andreas. Fjernt fra Danmark
Liszt, Franz (1811-1886). Apparitions; La bien-aimée;
    Carnival at Pest; Dante sonata; Marguerite and Armand;
    Mayerling; Transcendence; Vision of Marguerite
Lloyd, Norman (1909-   ). Lament for Ignacio Sánchez
    Mejías; La malinche
Loewe, Frederick (1904-   ). The Bitter Weird
Lolle, Jens. Amors og balletmestrens luner
Loomis, Harvey Worthington (1865-1930). Incense
Lovenskjold, Herman (1815-1870). La sylphide
Luciuk, Juliusz (1927-   ). Niobe; Pancernik Potiomkin
Ludt, Edvard Grieg. Haugtussa
Luigini, Alexandre (1850-1906). The Dance Dream
Lully, Jean-Baptiste (1632-1687). Les amants magnifiques;
    Le bourgeois gentilhomme; Cadmus et Hermione; Persée;
    Psyché; Le temple de la paix; Le triomphe de l'amour
Lumbye, Hans Christian (1810-1874). Drømmebilleder; Fjernt
    fra Danmark; Irene Holm; Napoli; Polka militaire; La
    ventana
Lutèce, Jean. Septuor
Lutoslawski, Witold (1913-   ). Mala suita

MacDowell, Edward (1860-1908). The Eagle
Macero, Teo (1925-   ). Opus 65; Session for Six
Machavriani, Aleksei (1913-   ). Otello
Magne, Michel (1930-   ). Le rendez-vous manque
Mahler, Gustav (1860-1911). At Midnight; Ce que l'amour me
    dit; Chant du compagnon errant; Dark Elegies; Epilogue;
    The Farewell; Gemini; Lied von der Erde; La rose
    malade; Shadow of the Wind; Traces
Maizel', Boris (1907-   ). A Distant Planet
Maklakiewicz, Jan Adam (1899-1954). Cagliostro w Warszawie;
    Zlota Kaczka
Malawski, Artur (1904-1957). Wierchy
Maliszewski, Witold (1873-1939). Boruta; Syrena
Malvezzi, Cristofano (1547-1599). La pellegrina
Manfredini, Vincenzo (1737-1799). Amour et Psyche
Mann, Herbie (1930-   ). Twice
Mannino, Franco (1924-   ). Mario e il mago
Marcus, Cara Bradbury. Orrenda
Marenco, Romualdo (1841-1907). Amor; Excelsior; Sieba;
    Sport
Marenzio, Luca (1554-1599). La pellegrina
Marliani, Marco Aurelio (1805-1849). La Gypsy.
Martin, Frank (1890-1974). Las hermanas; Laiderette

Martinů, Bohuslav (1890-1959). Anastasia; Ekon av
    trumpeter; Soldiers' Mass
Masekela, Hugh. Masekela Language
Massenet, Jules (1842-1912). Manon; Meditation; Meditation
    from "Thais"
Masson, Gérard (1936-   ). Lament of the Waves
Matsudaira, Yoritsune (1907-   ). Greek Dreams with Flute
Matushita, Chin-Ichi. Icarus
Mauduit, Jacques (1557-1627). Ballet de la délivrance de
    Renaud
Maurer, L. Wilhelm (1789-1878). L'ombre
Mayr, Simon (1763-1845). Kettentanz
Mayuzumi, Toshiro (1929-   ). Bagaku; Olympics
McBride, Robert. Show Piece
McCartney, Paul (1942-   ). Dance in Two Rows, Version III
McDowell, John Herbert. Insects and Heroes; Poet's
    Vaudeville
McFarland, Gary (1933-   ). Reflections in the Park
Medinš, Jānis (1890-1966). Le triomphe de l'amour
Meeker, Jess. Kinetic Molpai
Méhul, Etienne Nicholas (1763-1817). Dansomanie
Melikov, Arif (1933-   ). Legend of Love
Mendelssohn, Felix (1809-1847). Capriccio brillante; The
    Dream; Les elfes; Mendelssohn Symphony; A Midsummer
    Night's Dream; Scotch Symphony; Ein Sommernachtstraum;
    Spring Song
Menotti, Gian Carlo (1911-   ). Errand into the Maze;
    Sebastian; The Unicorn, the Gorgon, and the Manticore
Mercer, Johnny (1909-1976). Once More, Frank
Messager, André (1853-1929). Les deux pigeons
Métra, Olivier (1830-1899). Yedda
Meyerbeer, Giacomo (1791-1864). Gabriella di Vergy; Les
    patineurs
Meyrowitz, Walter. Egypta; The Yogi
Mignone, Francisco (1897-   ). Fantasia brasileira
Milhaud, Darius (1892-1974). The Bells; Le boeuf sur le
    toit; La création du monde; L'homme et son désir; The
    Maids; Les mariés de la Tour Eiffel; La rose des vents;
    Salade; Songes; Le train bleu
Milian, Jerzy. Tempus jazz 67
Miller, Freda. Fables for Our Time
Miller, Jay. Lunar Landing
Mingus, Charles (1922-1979). Blues for the Jungle
Minkus, Léon (1826-1917). La bayadère; Camargo; Don
    Quixote; Fiammetta; Kalkabrino; Notre Faust; La nuit et
    le jour; Paquita; Paquita pas de deux; Pas de trois; La
    source; Zoraiya

Mohaupt, Richard (1904-1957). Die Gaunerstreiche der
    Courasche; Max und Moritz
Mompou, Federico (1893-   ). House of Birds
Moniuszko, Stanislaw (1819-1872). Figle szatana; Na
    kwaterze
Monk, Meredith. (1942-   ). Juice; Triptych
Monteclair, Michel (1667-1737). Les tentations de la
    bergère
Monteverdi, Claudio (1567-1643). Il ballo delle ingrate; Il
    combattimento di Tancredi e Clorinda; From 1 to 10 to
    7; Tirsi e Clori
Morawski-Dabrowa, Eugeniusz (1876-1948). Switezianka
Morley, Thomas (d. 1602). The Consort
Moross, Jerome (1913-   ). Frankie and Johnny
Morozov, Igor. Doctor Aibolit
Mortifée, Ann. Ecstasy of Rita Joe
Morton, Jelly Roll (1885-1941). District Storyville; Eight
    Jelly Rolls
Mosolov, Alexander V. (1900-1973). Iron Foundry
Moszkowski, Moritz (1854-1925). Grand pas espagnol;
    Madroños
Moussorgsky, Modeste (1839-1881). David triomphant; The
    Fair at Sorochinsk; Le festin; La nuit sur le Mont
    Chauve; Pictures at an Exhibition
Mozart, Wolfgang Amadeus (1756-1791). Blow-out; Caracole;
    The Chase; Divertimento No. 15; Encounter; L'épreuve
    d'amour; Gartenfest; Graziana; Mozart Concerto;
    Pastorale; Les petits riens; Prometeo; Secret Places;
    Symphonie concertante
Muller, Jennifer. Nostalgia
Mumma, Gordon (1935-   ). Place
Munchheimer, Adam (1830-1904). Figle Szatana
Murgrave, Thea (1928-   ). Beauty and the Beast
Mushel', Geogiĭ (1909-   ). Balerina
Mussorgsky, Modest SEE Moussorgsky, Modeste

Nabokov, Nicolas (1903-1978). Don Quixote; Ode; Union
    Pacific
Nancarrow, Conlon (1912-   ). Crises
Neusiedler, Hans (1509-1563). The Consort
Nikolais, Alwin. Charade; Imago; Sanctum; Superantics '70;
    Tent; Tower
Nilsson, Bo (1937-   ). Nightwandering
Nobre, Marlos (1939-   ). Biosfera
Nono, Luigi (1924-   ). Genesis; Il mantello rosso; Der
    rote Mantel
Nordheim, Arne (1931-   ). Stages; The Tempest

Nordoff, Paul (1909-1977). Every Soul is a Circus
Nørgård, Per (1932-   ). Tango Chikane
North, Alex (1910-   ). A Streetcar Named Desire
Noskowski, Zygmunt (1846-1909). Świeto ognia
Nowak, Lionel (1911-   ). Flickers; A House Divided
Nowka, Dieter (1924-   ). Eine Bauernlegende
Nowowiejski, Feliks (1877-1946). Król Wichrów
Nyro, Laura. Quintet

Offenbach, Jacques (1819-1880). Bluebeard; Gaîté parisienne
    (1938); Gaîté parisienne (1978); Helen of Troy;
    Offenbach in the Underworld; Le papillon; Tales of
    Hoffmann
Ogerman, Claus. Some Times
Ohana, Maurice (1914-   ). Greek Dreams with Flute
Olatunji, Michael. Blues for the Jungle
Oldham, Arthur (1926-   ). Bonne-bouche; Mr. Punch; The
    Sailor's Return
Oransky, Valentin. The Merry Wives of Windsor
Oransky, Viktor. Futbolist; The Three Fat Men
Orff, Carl (1895-   ). Carmina Burana; Catulli Carmina
Orgad, Ben-Zion (1926-   ). One, Two, Three
Otkazov, F. The Bedbug

Pachelbel, Johann (1653-1706). Sacred Grove on Mount
    Tamalpais
Pacini, Giovanni (1796-1867). Le fée et le chevalier
Paganini, Niccolò (1782-1840). La fiancée du diable; The
    Mute Wife
Palester, Roman (1907-   ). Pieśń o ziemi
Palombo, Paul Martin. Et Cetera
Panizza, Giacomo (1804-1860). Faust; Ottaviano in Egitto
Parks, Carson C. Once More, Frank
Partos, Oedoen (1907-1977). Mythical Hunters
Paulli, Holger Simon (1810-1891). Blomsterfesten i Genzano;
    Kermessen i Brügge; Konservatoriet; Napoli
Pełko, Nikolaĭ (1916-   ). Joan of Arc
Penderecki, Krzysztof (1933-   ). Ceremony; H; Stabat
    mater
Pergolesi, Giovanni (1710-1736). Concertino in A Major;
    Pulcinella
Peri, Jacopo (1561-1633). La pellegrina
Perkowski, Piotr (1901-   ). Klementyna
Persius, Louis. Nina
Petit, Pierre (1922-   ). Ciné-bijou; Feux rouges, feux
    verts
Petrassi, Goffredo (1904-   ). La follia di Orlando; Le

Ravel, Maurice (1875–1937). Adélaïde; Alborada del
    gracioso; Une barque sur l'océan; Beauty and the Beast;
    Boléro; Chansons madécasses; Concerto in G; Daphnis et
    Chloé; L'enfant et les sortilèges; La fin du jour;
    Gaspard de la nuit; Introduction and Allegro for Harp;
    Ma mere l'oye; The Mermaid; Mother Goose Suite; Pavane;
    Promenade; Rapsodie espagnole; Sea Shadow; Shéhérazade;
    Sonatine; Tzigane; La valse; Vier mal vier; The Witch
Rawsthorne, Alan (1905–1971). Cage of God; Madame
    Chrysanthème
Reber, Napoléon–Henri (1807–1880). Le diable amoureaux
Reesen, Emil. Gaucho
Reich, Steve (1936–   ). Drumming; House; Square Dance
Reinhold, Otto (1899–1965). Die Nachtigall
Respighi, Ottorino (1879–1936). The Birds; Summer
    Interlude; Three Virgins and a Devil
Reutter, Hermann (1900–   ). Die Kirmes von Delft;
    Notturno Montmartre
Revil, Rudolf. Zodiac
Revueltas, Silvestre (1899–1940). Don Domingo
Reyer, Ernest (1823–1909). Sacountala
Ricci, José. Blues Suite
Richard, François (d. 1650). La douairière de Billebahaut
Richter, Marga (1926–   ). Abyss
Riegger, Wallingford (1885–1961). New Dance; A Poem
    Forgotten; Theatre Piece; Trend; With My Red Fires
Rieti, Vittorio (1898–   ). Le Bal; Barabau; Native
    Dancers; Night Shadow; The Triumph of Bacchus and
    Ariadne; Waltz Academy
Riisager, Knudåge (1897–1974). Etudes; Lady from the Sea;
    Månerenen; Qarrtsiluni; Tolv med posten
Rimsky-Korsakov, Nikolai (1844–1908). Capriccio espagnol;
    Cléopâtre; Le coq d'or; Le festin; Igrouchka;
    Shéhérazade; Le soleil de nuit
Rittman, Trude. The Bitter Weird; Charade; Four Marys
Rodgers, Richard (1902–1979). Ghost Town; Slaughter on
    Tenth Avenue
Rodolphe, Jean–Joseph (1730–1812). Médée et Jason
Rodrigo, Joaquín (1901–   ). Concierto de Aranjuez
Rogowski, Ludomir Michal (1881–1954). Bajka
Roland-Manuel (1891–1966). La guirlande de Campra
Rolla, Alessandro (1757–1841). Achille in Sciro
Romani, Felice (1788–1865). La fée et le chevalier
Romani, Pietro (1791–1877). Gabriella di Vergy
Ropartz, Joseph–Guy (1864–1955). L'indiscret
Rosenberg, Hilding (1892–   ). Adam och Eve
Rosenthal, Laurence (1926–   ). The Wind in the Mountains

Rossini, Gioacchino (1792–1868). La boutique fantasque; Con
    amore; Confetti; Divertimento; La fée et le chevalier;
    Gabriella di Vergy; L'île des pirates; Selina; Soirée
    musicale; William Tell Variations
Rota, Rinaldi (1911–1979). Amor di poeta; Le Molière
    imaginaire; La strada
Rouget de Lisle, Caude-Joseph (1760–1836). La marseillaise;
    Offrande à la liberté
Roussel, Albert (1869–1937). Bacchus et Ariane; Le festin
    de l'araignée; Padmâvatî
Różycki, Ludomir (1884–1953). Apollo i Dziewczyna; Pan
    Twardowski
Rubenstein, Anton (1829–1894). The Dance Dream; Katerina
Rugolo, Pete. Somnambulism; Strange Hero

Saint-Julien, Clémenceau de. La filleule des fées
Saint-Saëns, Camille (1835–1921). Carnival of Animals; The
    Dying Swan; Irish Fantasy; Javotte; Septet Extra
Sala, Oskar (1910–   ). Electronics
Salieri, Antonio (1750–1825). Apollo placato; Pafio e Mirra
Salmon, Jacques (1545– ?). Ballet comique de la Reine
Salzado, Leonard (1921–   ). The Fugitive; Hazard; Mardi
    Gras; The Witch Boy
Samuel, Gerhard (1924–   ). The Relativity of Icarus
Sanders, Robert (1906–1974). L'ag'ya
Santana. Twice
Satie, Erik (1866–1925). Esoterik Satie; Jack in the Box;
    Mercure; Monotones 1 and 2; Parade; Relâche; Squares
Sauguet, Henri (1901–   ). La chatte; Les forains; La
    guirlande de Campra; Les mirages; La nuit; La rencontre
Scarlatti, Domenico (1685–1787). Les comédiens jaloux; Les
    femmes de bonne humeur; Harlequin for President; Once
    Upon a Time; Piece Period; Der widerspenstigen Zähmung
Schaeffer, Pierre (1910–   ). Huescape; La symphonie pour
    un homme seul
Schall, Claus (1757–1835). Lagertha
Schenck, Johann (1753–1836). Bluebeard
Schiffman, Byron. Annabel Lee
Schilling, Otto-Erich. In scribo Satanis; Taubenflug
Schmidt, Harvey (1929–   ). Texas Fourth
Schmidt, Hermann. La Gitana
Schmitt, Florent (1870–1958). Oriane et la prince d'amour;
    Salomé; Un soir; Le tragédie de Salomé
Schneitzhoeffer, Jean-Madeleine (1785–1852). La sylphide
Schoenberg, Arnold (1874–1951). The Exiles; Imaginary Film;
    Opus 34; Pelléas et Mélisande; Pierrot lunaire; Pillar
    of Fire

Walden, Stanley (1932–   ). Weewis
Walton, William (1902–   ). Façade; The Quest
Ward-Steinman, David (1936–   ). These Three
Warlock, Peter (1894–1930). Capriol Suite
Warren, Harry (1893–   ). Notre Faust
Watson, Gwendolyn. Poison Variations
Weber, Carl Maria von (1786–1826). Pas de deux romantique;
     Le spectre de la rose; The Thief Who Loved a Ghost;
     Vienna 1814
Webern, Anton (1883–1945). Episodes; Incubus; Moments; Opus
     I
Weigl, Joseph (1766–1840). Prometeo
Weill, Kurt (1900–1950). The Judgement of Paris; Les septs
     péchés capitaux
Weinberger, Jaromir (1896–1967). Saratoga
Wenzel, Leopold (1847–1925). Les papillons; The Press
Whyte, Ian (1901–1960). Donald of the Burthens
Widor, Charles Marie (1844–1937). La Korrigane
Wilder, Alec (1907–   ). Juke Box
Williams, Zoe. The Lonely Ones
Williamson, Malcolm (1931–   ). Sinfonietta; Sun into
     Darkness
Wimberger, Gerhard (1923–   ). Der Hanschuh
Wiszniewski, Zbigniew (1922–   ). Ad Hominem
Wodynski, Mike. Changeover
Wolff, Christian (1934–   ). Changing Steps
Woloshin, Sid (1928–   ). PAMTGG
Woźniak, Franciszek. Wariacje 4 : 4

Xenakis, Iannis (1922–   ). Metastaseis & Pithoprakta;
     Nomus alpha; Orient-Occident; Private Domain

Young, La Monte (1938–   ). Winterbranch
Yurovsky, Vladimir. Crimson Sails
Yvain, Maurice (1891–1965). Blanche-neige

Zalamea, Janet. Juice
Zimmermann, Bernd Alois (1918–1970). Présence
Zlatin, Mois. Voices of Spring